# THE **TESTING** SERIES

# PARACHUTE REGIMENT OFFICER

## **PASSING** THE SELECTION PROCESS

# THE **TESTING** SERIES
*expert advice on interview preparation*

how2become

Orders: Please contact How2become Ltd, Suite 2, 50 Churchill Square Business Centre, Kings Hill, Kent ME19 4YU.

Please order via the email address: info@how2become.co.uk.

ISBN: 9781907558825

First published 2012

Typeset for How2become Ltd by Molly Hill, Canada.

Printed in Great Britain for How2become Ltd by
Bell & Bain Ltd, 303 Burnfield Road, Thornliebank, Glasgow G46 7UQ.

# CONTENTS

# ARMY OFFICER TRAINING COURSE

Do you want to attend a 1 Day Army Officer AOSB preparation training course?

Visit the following website to find out more:

**ArmyOfficerCourse.co.uk**

# WELCOME

Welcome to your new guide – How to pass the Parachute Regiment Officer selection process. This guide has been designed to help you prepare for, and pass the Parachute Regiment Officer selection process, including the Army Officer Selection Board (AOSB).

The author of this guide, Richard McMunn, has spent over 20 years in both the Armed Forces and the Emergency Services. He has vast experience and knowledge in the area of Armed Forces recruitment and you will find his guidance both inspiring and highly informative. During his successful career in the Fire Service Richard sat on many interview panels assessing candidate's to join the job. He has also been extremely successful at passing job interviews and assessments himself and has a success rate of over 90%. Follow his advice and preparation techniques carefully and you too can achieve the same levels of success in your career.

Whilst the selection process for joining the Parachute Regiment as an Officer is highly competitive, there are a number of things you can do in order to improve your chances of success, and they are all contained within this guide.

The guide itself has been split up into useful sections to make it easier for you to prepare for each stage. Read each section carefully and take notes as you progress. Don't ever give up on your dreams; if you really want to become a Parachute Regiment Officer then you can do it. The way to prepare for a job in the Armed Forces as an Officer is to embark on a programme of 'in-depth' preparation, and this guide will show you exactly how to do just that.

If you need any further help with the selection tests, planning exercises, getting fit or Parachute Regiment Officer interview advice, then we offer a wide range of courses, books and DVD products to assist you. These are all available through our online shop www.how2become.co.uk.

We are also now running a number of 1 Day Army Officer Selection Board preparation training courses at the following link:

**www.ArmyOfficerCourse.co.uk**

Once again, thank you for your custom and we wish you every success in your pursuit to joining the Parachute Regiment as an Officer.

Work hard, stay focused and be what you want…

Best wishes,

*The how2become team*

The How2become Team

# PREFACE
## BY RICHARD MCMUNN

I spent four years of my life in the Armed Forces from the age of 17 to 21. During these four years I experienced some of the best moments of my life. My career in the Armed Forces taught me how to be disciplined, it taught me how to be organised and it also provided me with a sound footing for a successful future. But it didn't start out all plain sailing. I initially failed the selection process for the Armed Forces by failing the medical due to being overweight. I can remember sitting in the Armed Forces careers office in Preston, Lancashire at the age of 16 waiting patiently to see the Warrant Officer who would interview me as part of my application for joining. I had already passed the written tests, and despite never having sat an interview before in my life, I was confident of success.

In the build up to the interview I had worked very hard studying the job that I was applying for, and also working hard on my interview technique. At the end of the interview I was told that I had easily passed and all that was left to complete was the medical. Unfortunately I was overweight at the time and I was worried that I might fail. At the medical my fears became a reality and I was told by the doctor that I would have to lose a stone in weight before they would accept me. I walked out of the doctor's surgery and began to walk to the bus stop that would take me back home three miles away. I was absolutely gutted, and embarrassed, that I had failed at the final hurdle, all because I was overweight!

I sat at the bus stop feeling sorry for myself and wondering what job I was going to apply for next. My dream of joining the Armed Forces was over and I didn't know which way to turn. Suddenly, I began to feel a sense of determination to lose the weight and get fit in the shortest time possible. It was at that particular point in my life when things would change forever. As the bus approached I remember thinking there was no time like the present for getting started on my fitness regime. I therefore opted to walk the three miles home instead of being lazy and getting the bus. When I got home I sat in my room and wrote out a 'plan of action' that would dictate how I was going to lose the weight required. That plan of action was very simple and it said the following three things:

1. Every weekday morning I will get up at 6am and run 3 miles.

2. Instead of catching the bus to college, and then back home again, I will walk.

3. I will eat healthily and I will not go over the recommended daily calorific intake.

Every day I would read my simple 'action plan' and it acted as a reminder of what I needed to do. Within a few weeks of following my plan rigidly I had lost over a stone in weight and I was a lot fitter too!

When I returned back to the doctor's surgery for my medical the doctor was amazed that I had managed to lose the weight in such a short space of time and he was pleased that I had been so determined to pass the medical. Six months later I started my basic training course with a big smile on my face!

Ever since then I have always made sure that I prepare properly for any job application. If I do fail a particular interview or section of an application process then I will always go out of my way to ask for feedback so that I can improve for next time. I also still use an 'action plan' in just about every element of my work today. Action plans allow you to focus your mind on what you want to achieve and I would strongly recommend that you use one during your preparation for the Parachute Regiment Officer Selection process.

Throughout my career I have always been successful. It's not because I am better than the next person, but simply because I prepare better. I didn't do very well at school so I have to work a lot harder to pass the exams and written tests that form part of a job application process, but I am always aware of what I need to do and what I must improve on.

I have always been a great believer in preparation. Preparation was my key to success, and it also yours. Without the right level of preparation you will be setting out on the route to failure. The Parachute Regiment is hard to join as an Officer, but if you follow the steps that I have compiled within this guide and use them as part of your preparation, then you will increase your chances of success dramatically.

The men and women of the Armed Forces carry out an amazing job. They are there to protect us and our country and they do that job with great pride, passion and very high levels of professionalism and commitment. They are to be congratulated for the job that they do. Before you apply to join the Paras as an Officer you need to be fully confident that you too are capable of providing that same level of commitment. If you think you can do it, and you can rise to the challenge, then you just might be the type of person the Army is looking for.

Best wishes,

*Richard McMunn*

Richard McMunn

# CHAPTER 1

# THE QUALITIES REQUIRED TO BECOME A PARACHUTE REGIMENT OFFICER IN THE ARMY

Before I get into the selection process and the different elements of the Army Officer Selection Board I want to go into detail about the qualities that are required to become an Officer. The reason for this is simple; I want you to concentrate on demonstrating these throughout the duration of the selection process. If you demonstrate these then your chances of success will increase dramatically.

Many candidates who attend the Potential Officers Insight Course (POIC) and the Army Officer Selection Board (AOSB) will be under prepared. In addition to this many candidates will spend hours scouring internet chat forums in an attempt to find hints and tips on how to pass the AOSB. Whilst there is nothing wrong with this, the most effectively prepared candidates are those who concentrate primarily on demonstrating the key assessable qualities in order to become an Officer in the Parachute Regiment. You certainly do not need me to tell you that physical fitness will have a huge influence in your ability to pass; you should already know this. Be sure to dedicate enough time on your fitness but conversely, do not neglect the other important areas of preparation, and in particular, the qualities of an Officer.

The whole purpose of the POIC and the AOSB is to determine whether or not you have the 'potential' to become an Officer in the Parachute Regiment. If you have the potential then there is a greater chance that you will pass Officer Initial Training course at Sandhurst. The Army will be investing literally hundreds of thousands of pounds into your development and career progression. Therefore, they want to be sure that you have the potential to pass every stage of training.

In order to assess the potential the Army will assess you against a series of qualities and competencies. Before I move on to the scoring criteria I want to talk a little about the qualities that you need to demonstrate during the entire selection process, and these include the POIC and the AOSB. You will notice that after each list of qualities I have provided you with some useful tips.

## QUALITIES THAT YOU NEED TO DEMONSTRATE

- Determined
- Resolute
- Persistent
- Unwavering
- Steady
- Able to overcome most difficulties
- Strong-willed.

**TIPS:** You are applying to join the Paras as an Officer. Therefore, it is crucial that you are able to remain calm in a crisis, be totally focused on achieving the end result and be determined to succeed at everything you do.

For example, during the planning exercise stage, which is probably the toughest part of the AOSB, you will be placed under considerable pressure by the assessing Officer's. If you do not know the answer to a question then it is better to say so, rather than panic, waffle or crumble under the pressure. One of the main purposes of AOSB is to determine whether or not you have the ability to stay focused under pressure.

- Imaginative
- Initiative
- Constructive
- Perceptive
- Original
- Mentally agile

- Inventive
- Visionary
- Intelligent
- Mature
- Balanced.

*Tips:* These qualities are predominantly focused on your state of mind. Do you have the ability to come up with solutions to problems? Can you think outside the box? Can you see the end result? Are you sensible and mature for your years? During every stage of the POIC and the AOSB make sure you remain level-headed. Do not act in a foolhardy way and always think before you speak. Engage your brain before you engage your mouth!

- Forceful
- Compelling
- Persuasive
- Powerful
- Vigorous
- Assertive
- Consistent

- Effective
- Resourceful
- Magnetic
- Inspiring
- Considerate
- Considerable impact.

**TIPS:**  Let us assume that you are participating in the Planning Exercise phase. You have worked hard during your preparation in the build up to AOSB and you are very confident that your plan of tackling the exercise is the most effective. However, two other members of your group have alternative solutions to the problem. What do you do? The options are simple – you can either go along with their desired solutions(s) or you can have the confidence in your own abilities and your plan and attempt to 'persuade' them both that your option is the most effective. If I was attending AOSB, I would have the confidence in my own abilities and persuade them that my option is the most effective.

**Remember** – you are applying to become a Parachute Regiment Officer and that means you are applying to become a leader!

- Bold

- Daring

- Courageous
- Entrepreneurial
- Enthusiastic
- Spirit of adventure
- Untiring
- Energetic
- Active

- Diligent
- Industrious
- Persevering
- Physically strong and active
- Organiser
- Sense of urgency.

**TIPS:** During Command Tasks that form part of the POIC and the AOSB be sure to get involved. Those people, who believe that if they sit on the fence and don't get involved will go unnoticed, are sorely mistaken. You must get involved, come up with solutions, encourage the team, support others and try your hardest to achieve every task that you are set. When it is your turn to take command, do so. Do not be weak; be strong, confident and in control at all times; more on this later. Above all, do not be selfish during the Command Tasks. Help out your team-mates and focus on achieving the task in hand.

- Tolerant
- Flexible
- Co-operative
- Diplomatic

- Tactful
- Resilient (never gives in)
- Adaptable
- Willing to accept responsibility.

**TIPS:** What are you like towards other people? Do you have the ability to work with others as part of a team? Every team encounters problems along the way. How you deal with those problems is what matters. Be tolerant of other people, always be flexible in your approach to tasks, never give in and be the first to put your hand up when they ask for a volunteer.

- Sensible
- Respective
- Shrewd
- Well-balanced
- Decisive

- Discerning
- Fair
- Unbiased
- Loyal
- Steadfast.

I have now provided you with plenty of qualities that all go towards making an effective Officer in the Parachute Regiment. So, when the interview panel asks you the question "What are the qualities of an Officer?" you will have no problem answering it!

## YOU ARE A LEADER AND A MANAGER

Parachute Regiment Officers are both leaders and managers. Therefore, it is important that you understand the difference between each of them and how they are interlinked.

In order to become a competent Officer you will need to be effective at both. Here's a brief explanation of how they differ:

**Leader** – A leader is someone who effectively takes a team of people from point A to point B. These two 'points' don't have to be in terms of distance, but instead they could be a mission or a company or organisational goal. For example, it might be a football manager attempting to lead his or her team to promotion to a higher league. A leader should be a visionary. They should 'see' where they want their team to be and take steps to get them there.

**Manager** – A manager is someone who arranges and uses resources in order to achieve a companies or organisations goal. Examples of resources are:

• People

• Utilities such as water, gas and electricity

• Vehicles and equipment

• Paper and pencils

• Fuel

• Time

An effective manager will use his or her resources effectively. They will not waste resources and they will use them appropriately. A manager's greatest asset is his people whom which he commands. When you join the Paras as an Officer you will undoubtedly be responsible at some point in your career for a group or team of people. How you manage them is very important.

## HOW DO THEY WORK TOGETHER?

During my time in the Fire Service I served as an Officer for many years. Without wishing to blow my own trumpet, I was a highly effective manager and leader. Managerial and leadership skills are interlinked and you will draw on each of these assets at different times during your career as an

Officer in the Paras. For example, whilst attending severe fires and road traffic collisions in the Fire Service, I was required to use both leadership and managerial skills at the same time in order to achieve the required task. I would always have a plan that was discussed with my Junior Officers. I would assign people and equipment (resources) to carry out certain tasks at the incident. I would order equipment, fuel and refreshments (resources) well in advance of them running out. I would arrange many hours in advance for relief crews to attend the incident in order to replace my tiring firefighters. I would support my team and I would communicate effectively with them during every stage of the incident. At the end of the incident I would always hold an incident debrief. This would allow me to thank everyone for their efforts and allow us to identify any areas of improvement for future incidents.

All of these actions were using my 'managerial' skills. In terms of leadership skills, I would brief my team well in order to explain the plan and what it was that needed to be done. I would provide words of support and encouragement throughout the operation and I would listen carefully to my junior officer's advice and suggestions during every stage of the incident.

Being an Officer in the Paras is about drawing on different skills and assets in order to achieve a task or goal. That goal may take many years to achieve and may not necessarily be a short term objective. Always remember that in order to become a competent Officer, you will need to be an effective leader and manager.

# CHAPTER 2

# THE SELECTION PROCESS FOR BECOMING A PARACHUTE REGIMENT OFFICER

The majority of people who will read this guide will have a thorough understanding of what the selection process consists of. Before I get into each element of selection however, and more importantly how to pass them, it is important for me to briefly explain the different elements.

To begin with, applicants will need to contact their local Armed Forces Careers Office and explain that they wish to apply to become an Officer with the Parachute Regiment. The most effective way to do this is to go along to your nearest centre for a brief chat. You will be supplied with an information pack and details on how to apply, providing you meet the minimum eligibility requirements.

You can also research the different jobs that are available as an officer by using the Army's online job explorer. This can be found by visiting the Army website at: **www.army.mod.uk**

## THE ARMY CAREERS ADVISOR INTERVIEW

You will eventually be invited to attend what is called the Army Careers Advisor (ACA) interview. Sometimes this interview is referred to as the AFCO interview or the 'filter' interview. This interview is designed to assess whether or not you have the right qualities to become an Officer in the Parachute Regiment and it is also the opportunity for you to decide whether or not the Army is for you. If you successfully pass the ACA interview and a medical check, you will be put forward to attend the Potential Officers Insight Course, or POIC as it is commonly referred to. POIC candidates will be required to undergo a number of individual tests (in which they are expected to show both mental and physical robustness) and team tasks (to evaluate their leadership potential).

Candidates will be provided with feedback on their performance and advised on areas which need further development, if they are to be successful in their pursuit of a Commission in The Parachute Regiment. There are only a few Commissions available in the Regiment each year and competition is fierce.

The ACA interview is, in my opinion, relatively easy to pass. However, you will still need to put in plenty of preparation and I have provided you with a host of sample questions and responses during a later section of this guide. If you successfully pass the POIC you will be required to attend two Boards. The first is an AOSB briefing and the second is the Main Board.

## THE AOSB BRIEFING

The AOSB briefing is 2 days in duration and is held at the Westbury. During your stay here you will be assessed on:

**1.** Your physical ability;

**2.** Practical ability;

**3.** Teamwork ability;

**4.** Leadership ability.

The briefing is also an opportunity for you to see whether Army life is for you and to also prepare for the full AOSB Main Board. During the briefing you will get to try many of the elements that you'll be assessed against during the Main Board, such as:

- An opening discussion with the other candidates
- Aptitude tests – verbal reasoning, numerical reasoning and abstract reasoning
- Planning exercise
- Practical techniques
- Physical fitness tests including the bleep test and an obstacle course

I have provided you with lots of free resources to assist you for the aptitude tests at the following link:

**www.ArmyOfficerTests.co.uk**

Once the briefing is complete the assessors will get together and discuss your performance. You will be placed in one of the four categories:

**CATEGORY 1** – Invited to attend the AOSB Main Board.

**CATEGORY 2** – You will be invited to attend AOSB Main Board after a set period of time during which you will be required to work on your weaker areas.

**CATEGORY 3** – The board believes that you will fail Main Board. However, you can attend if you wish to do so.

**CATEGORY 4** – Unsuitable for AOSB Main Board.

As you can see, it is important to aim for CATEGORY 1 or CATEGORY 2 at the very least. If you achieve CATEGORY 1 then you will normally be invited back to Westbury within 8 weeks. During this 8 week period it is vital that you continue your preparation. Passing the briefing is by no means an indication that you will pass the Main Board.

## THE AOSB MAIN BOARD

The AOSB Main Board takes place at Westbury. Boards usually run during the week, however, there are weekend boards for those people who cannot genuinely attend during the week.

At each Main Board there will normally be up to 40 people attending both male and female. You will be split up into medium sized groups of approximately 8 people for the duration of the board. Groups will consist of men and women of a variety of different ages. This is done deliberately, to assess whether or not you can work with people of the opposite sex and also with people whom are younger and older than you.

You will be assessed against a number of different areas which I will explain later on in a different section of this guide.

The AOSB Main Board is designed to assess whether or not you have the right personal qualities and attributes to become a successful Officer. The only way you will pass it is through hard work and determination.

There are two key elements to passing the AOSB –

**1.** How you perform

**2.** How you behave

Whilst there are many different factors that can influence each element, they both must be taken seriously. For example, you will be required to work in groups of up to 8 people. How you treat each member of your group, both as a team player and a team leader will be assessed. You will also be assessed on your attitude. If you are cocky, arrogant, dismissive, or you have a negative attitude towards discipline, then you will not pass the board.

The assessors will naturally expect you to have found out as much as you can about the Army, its history, its mission, its equipment, weapons, tanks and aircraft, and they will also ask you questions about the training you would expect to go through if you are successful as an Officer. There is plenty of hard work ahead of you if you want to pass the AOSB Main Board, but the hard work will certainly be worth it!

During the Main Board you will be required to undergo the following key assessable areas:

## DAY 1

*Fitness tests:* These will be carried out shortly after you arrive at the AOSB and you will be required to undertake the bleep test, the exact same test as the briefing. You will be expected to achieve level 10. If you fail to achieve the minimum standard then it is highly likely that you will be asked to leave the board. Anyone who cannot reach this standard before they arrive at board is, in my opinion, plain stupid. You know before you attend the Main Board what the standard is, therefore, you should be able to achieve it with great ease. If you do not have a copy of the bleep test then you can obtain one right now at:

**www.how2become.co.uk**

Do not leave it until the last minute to practice, start working on your fitness now.

*Essay and General Knowledge tests:* Following the brief by the assessing staff you will be required to write an essay based on a specific topic that is usually centered on current affairs. Many people score poorly on the written essay, simply because they fail to put in any practice before the main board.  Following the essay you will be required to sit the following computer based tests:

• General knowledge

• Army/Service knowledge

• Current affairs

In my opinion, the Army/Service knowledge test questions can be prepared for. However, the general knowledge questions that you will encounter from the test will be extremely diverse in nature. I am not saying that you shouldn't prepare for this part of the test; however, personally I would spend more time concentrating on the other two elements during my preparation time.

## Examples of Army/Service Knowledge Questions

As part of your preparation, go away and find out the answer to each of the following questions.

1.  Troops fighting on the front line are issued with CBA. What does CBA stand for?

2.  What is the rank badge of Staff Sergeant?

3.  The L129A1 Sharpshooter rifle fires what size round?

4.  Which insignia denotes a Lieutenant General?

5.  What does N.A.T.O stand for?

6.  How much is the annual Army Budget?

7.  What is the highest commissioned rank of the Army?

8.  What is the highest non-commissioned rank of the Army?

9.  The Mk 6 Assault Boat is constructed from what metal?

10. The Combat Support Boat is used exclusively by which Corps?

11. How many countries are in NATO?

12. Name all of the UK Army bases?

13. What is the name of the military operations in Afghanistan?

14. What is the purpose of the Army's Logistic Vehicles?

15. The ATMP is a versatile, lightweight load-carrying vehicle used by airborne and air-mobile battalions. What does ATMP stand for?

16. DROPS vehicles form the logistic backbone of the British Army. What does DROPS stand for?

17. Name 5 types of Protected Patrol Vehicles?

18. How many Army personnel are there approximately?

19. The Defender is the latest version of the Islander twin turboprop aircraft. What is its gross weight?

20. What is the maximum speed in knots of the Gazelle helicopter?

21. What does CBRN stand for?

22. The Light Role Team (LRT) Is the United Kingdom's early entry capability for CBRN. They provide Detection, Identification, Monitoring and what two other functions?

23. Who is the current Commander-in-Chief Land Forces?

24. The Commander-in-Chief Land Forces reports directly to whom?

25. The Starstreak HVM is designed to counter threats from very high performance, low-flying aircraft. What does HVM stand for?

26. The Rapier Field Standard C is a technologically advanced SHORAD. What does SHORAD stand for?

27. Officer Initial Training takes place where?

28. The Commissioning Course for Regular Army Officers, including recess periods, is how long?

29. The GMLRS provides pinpoint accuracy delivering a 200lb high explosive warhead to its target. What does GMLRS stand for?

30. Who is the current Chief of the General Staff?

The above 30 questions are just a small sample of the type of question you will encounter. I would recommend spending plenty of time studying the Army website during your preparation. Not only will this help you during the computer-based tests but it will also assist you during the interviews. I would also recommend you obtain a copy of the following book from Amazon and all good bookstores as it contains a wealth of information relating to the British Army: *The British Army: A Pocket Guide*

## ESSAY WRITING TIPS

1.  For the introduction, write the thesis statement and give some background information. The thesis statement is put into the essay introduction and it should reveal your point of view on the matter, or position you intend to support in your paper.

2.  Develop each supporting paragraph and make sure to follow the correct format.

3.  Write clear and simple sentences to express your meaning.

4.  Focus on the main idea of your essay.

5.  Consider using a well structured format for you essay such as:

    **Beginning** – Include the thesis statement and background information.

    **Middle** – This will be the main part of the essay and will include your argument, the reasons for it and any supporting evidence or information.

    **End** – Conclude and summarise.

*Try writing an essay on any of the following topics:*

1.  Politicians too often base their decisions on what will please the voters, not on what is best for the country.

2.  Wealthy politicians cannot offer fair representation to all the people.

3.  In a free society, laws must be subject to change.

4.  An understanding of the past is necessary for solving the problems of the present.

5.  Education comes not from books but from practical experience.

6.  Is climate change man-made?

7.  Should the death penalty be re-introduced?

8.  Is the current electoral system fair?

9.  Is torture ever acceptable in today's world?

10. Is it right that men should get paternity leave from work?

11. Is the UK taxation system fair?

12. Are we too reliant on computers and the internet?

13. Should we use animals for research?

14. Should the UK government have a say in what we eat and drink?

15. Does access to condoms prevent teenage pregnancy and sexually transmitted diseases?

## DAY 2

The Opening Discussion: At the beginning of day 2 you will be required to undertake a group discussion. This part of the assessment will last for approximately 40 minutes, during which time you will be required to discuss a number of different topics with the other members of your group. The most effective way to prepare for this part of the AOSB is to:

1.  Have an excellent knowledge of current affairs

2.  Be a good communicator verbally

3.  Be a good listener

The group opening discussion element of the AOSB is designed to assess your ability to communicate and interact with other people. As you are already aware, Officers are required to communicate, and discuss topical issues with other members of the Army. In addition to this they must have the intellect to converse with agencies outside of the Armed Forces as well as their colleagues from the RAF and the Royal Navy. This part of the assessment will determine your ability to do just that.

There will be up to eight people in the discussion which will be a mix of ages and genders. It is important that you can get on with everyone, regardless of their age, background, religious beliefs or sexual orientation. Before I provide you with some tips on how to score high during the group opening discussion, let us first take a look at three important assessable areas:

• Confidence and Resilience

- Oral Communication

- Influence

Many candidates believe that all you need to do during the discussion in order to score well is to contribute to the discussion. This couldn't be further from the truth. Yes, it is imperative that you get involved and have an opinion, but you must concentrate on other areas too, such as your ability to listen to others and involve others in the conversation. You will see that one of the assessable areas is that of 'influence'. During the discussion, you may be presented with a situation where the other members of the group disagree with your opinion or view. Whilst that is fine and acceptable, would you be able to influence them and change their mind about your views?

Here are a number of important tips that will help you score high during the group discussion.

**TIP 1** – Whilst in the chair, sit up-right and do not slouch or lean forward. Sit with your legs uncrossed and rest your palms on your knees. Whilst you should not sit rigid, you should look presentable.

**TIP 2** – There will be a number of discussions to be had. In total the discussion session will last for approximately 40 minutes, so there is ample time for you to get involved and score high. Try starting off a few discussions. Don't just leave it to the other members of the group to start off the topic. Remember, one of the assessable areas is that of confidence and resilience.

If you are struggling to think of anything to say for a specific topic, you could start off the conversation by saying:

*"Does anybody have any strong views on this topic?"*

By saying this, you will be actively involved in the conversation and you will be also involving others into the conversation.

**TIP 3** – When you have finished contributing to the debate, try and involve another person into the conversation. For example:

*"That's my view on this subject, what do you think?"*

Once again you will score higher marks for actively involving others into the conversation.

**TIP 4** – Involve other people who have not yet had chance to speak. If you notice a member of the group struggling to get their opinion heard, try saying something like:

*"I notice you haven't had the chance to say anything yet, what's your view on this subject?"*

**TIP 5** – Actively demonstrate good listening skills. This is the part that many people are poor at. Once they have finished speaking, they sit back and wait for their turn to speak again. Avoid this at all costs! I strongly recommend that you show active listening skills when other people in the group are speaking. Nod your head and use facial expressions to demonstrate that you are still involved in the topic of conversation.

**TIP 6** – Be careful what you say! Over the past few years I have run a number of 1 day Army Officer training courses that help people prepare for their AOSB. During the course we run through a number of group opening discussions. During every session, someone is guaranteed to say something that will probably give them an automatic fail for the entire AOSB. Sometimes people have a tendency to say something controversial; albeit they probably didn't intend to. My advice is this – it is important that you get involved during the discussions, and even more important that you have an opinion and don't sit on the fence, however, you must think before you speak. If you believe that what you will say might be taken in the wrong way, avoid saying it.

**TIP 7** – Speak clearly and concisely. During the group opening discussion be clear in what you say, speak up and avoid hesitations such as *'erm'* or *'agh'*. In addition to other areas, you are being assessed on your oral communication skills.

**TIP 8** – Have a number of topics that you can start off a discussion with. Although it is more probable that the assessing staff will provide you the topics to discuss, they may also ask you to come up with topics yourself. Therefore, before you attend AOSB, pick 5 subjects that you can use during the group discussions phase.

Now let's take a look at a number of sample topics that have been used in the past.

## SAMPLE GROUP DISCUSSION TOPICS

• Should women be allowed to join the Armed Forces?

- Was Hitler a good leader?
- What do you think about gay people being allowed to join the Armed Forces?
- Speeding cameras are a total waste of time – discuss.
- How could the use and popularity of public transport be increased within this country?
- Professional footballers. Are they overpaid?
- Is the increase in overseas football club owners good for the sport?
- The pros and cons of having a credit card.
- Marijuana has a medical value.
- The pros and cons of a female President.
- Should schools distribute condoms?
- Life imprisonment is a good alternative to capital punishment.
- What makes a good leader?
- Was the Iraq war a waste of time?
- What should Britain's place in Europe be?
- Is modern technology changing the way we communicate for the better?
- Should smoking have been banned in public places?
- Is animal testing defensible in modern society?
- Should the public be concerned about the increasing use of DNA technology?
- Should people be required to opt out of organ donation rather than opt in?
- How could more people be encouraged to vote?
- Can the salaries of professional football players be justified?
- Should the private life of celebrities come under so much scrutiny?
- Do we need to change the attitude of car drivers towards speed limits?
- Should our police officers be routinely armed?
- Should we be worried about obesity?
- Should organised team sport be included in the national curriculum?

- Should there be a compulsory retirement age?
- Do we need to change Britain's drinking culture?
- Should there be any limitations to the treatment available on the NHS?
- Has the National Lottery been good for Britain?
- Should the BBC be funded by a license fee?

*Numerous interviews:* All candidates who attend the AOSB Main Board will be required to sit interviews with the Vice President, Deputy President and Education Adviser.

I have dedicated an entire section to the AOSB interviews in a later section of this guide.

*Outdoor tasks:* The outdoor tasks are normally carried out after lunch on the second day. Therefore, it is important that you don't eat a 'heavy' meal. Eat something that is packed full of carbohydrates and also remember to drink plenty of water.

The outdoor task is basically a 'leaderless' task, which means there is no designated leader. An example of a task might be where you are required to get from point A to B without touching the floor and whilst carrying a heavy object such as a large metal drum or heavy ammunition box.

Once again, I have dedicated a chapter to the outdoor task later on in this guide.

Once the outdoor task is complete you will be required to compete against the other groups in a leaderless task. During this part of the assessment, which is called the opening race, you will be assessed against your overall effort, teamwork ability, potential leadership and problem solving skills.

Planning exercise tutorial: The final part of the second day will see you receive a planning exercise tutorial in preparation for the following day's assessment. As previously mentioned, it is my personal belief that the Planning Exercise is the hardest part of the entire AOSB. I have dedicated an entire section of this guide to the Plan Ex.

## DAY 3

*Planning exercise:* At the commencement of day 3 you will be required to take part in the planning exercise. This is a theoretical written exercise which will assess your ability to use time, resources and people in an effective and efficient manner. You will be provided with a written brief relating to a fictitious scenario. You will also be provided with a map to study that is relative to the brief. You will have an hour to read, study and analyse the brief and come up with your own solution to the problem. Once the hour is complete, you will then be required to discuss the scenario with your group in order to come up with an agreed solution to the problem.

You will be assessed against how you contribute to the discussion and also how you react to the ideas of others within your group.

Once the group discussion element is complete, you will be required to answer questions on your decisions by the assessing Officers. I have dedicated an entire section of this guide to the planning exercise later on.

*Outdoor Command tasks:* Following the planning exercise stage you will then be required to take command of a group of people. When it is not your turn to be in command, you will be required to act as a team member. The leader of the group will brief you and then allow you just a few minutes to develop your plan. You will then be required to explain the plan to your group before executing it.

Once again I have dedicated an entire section to the outdoor command task in a later chapter of this guide.

*Obstacle course:* The final task of the morning on day three is the individual obstacle course. You will be required to negotiate an obstacle course with the object of completing as many obstacles as possible within a set time limit.

*Lecturette:* In the afternoon of day 3 you will be required to give a 5 minute talk to the rest of the group on a subject that is chosen from your CV. You will have 5 subjects to choose from and you will be given a set time period to prepare. However, it is my strong advice that you study your CV and practice giving a presentation, before you attend the AOSB. Once the 5 minute period is complete you will then be required to answer questions from your group. The lecturette is designed to assess your ability and confidence when talking in front of a group of people.

*Dinner:* In the evening of day 3 you will enjoy a formal dinner the rest of the candidates. Whilst the Army will tell you that this activity is not assessed, remember that they will not score your performance until the following day. Don't get drunk, don't show off and don't make a fool of yourself!

## DAY 4

*Final race:* During the morning of the final day you will take part in what is called the final race. This is an outdoor leaderless task that will see your group go up against the other groups in a race to finish an obstacle course. This is your final chance to really show the assessing officers how good you are.

Immediately following the final race the board will meet up to discuss your performance. The board take this part extremely serious and the comments made by the Group Leader, the Deputy President and the Education Adviser will be analysed and discussed in depth. The results of your board will be sent out to you that day and will normally take just 2-3 days to arrive.

Now that we understand what the selection process consists of, let's take a look at the scoring criteria.

# CHAPTER 3
# THE SELECTION PROCESS SCORING CRITERIA

Within this I section of the guide I will provide you with information that relates to how the Army will assess you during the entire Officer selection process. During the second section of this chapter I will provide you with information that is relative to the AOSB scoring criteria.

The criteria that I am going to provide you with during this first section relates to your own personal attributes, qualities and also your knowledge of the Army and your chosen career as an Officer in the Parachute Regiment. This information will act as a very good foundation for your preparation and you should learn it before you attend the initial ACA interview. If you are capable of providing the Army Selecting Officers with what they are looking for then your chances of success will greatly increase.

The marking sheet used to assess your abilities covers a number of different assessable areas. The following list is a selection of some of the criteria used:

- Personal turnout;
- Sociability;
- Emotional maturity and stability;
- Drive and determination to succeed;
- Physically robust;
- Experience of being self-reliant;
- Reactions to social discipline;
- Experience of and reaction to regimentation and routine;
- Knowledge and experience of Army life;
- Motivation to join the Parachute Regiment;
- Reasons for wanting to join as an Officer;
- Experience of leadership;
- Personal circumstances.

This list is not exhaustive and there will be other areas that the Army will be assessing you on during the initial ACA interview. However, having an understanding of the qualities you need to demonstrate throughout selection will improve your chances of success dramatically.

In order to provide you with a greater understanding of what is required I will now go into more detail about each specific area.

## PERSONAL TURNOUT

The Army are looking for you to be smartly dressed when you attend the AFCO for your ACA interview. Try to think of how you would expect a Parachute Regiment Officer to present themselves. You would expect them to be smart, formal and professional. When you attend the careers office, whether it is for an interview or a careers presentation, always make sure you wear a formal outfit such as a suit or shirt and tie. Whilst this is not essential, it will allow you to score higher in the area of 'personal turnout'.

Many people will stroll into the careers office wearing jeans and trainers. Make an effort to stand out for the right reasons and this certainly will work in your favour. Those people who turn up to the Armed Forces Careers Office dressed untidy and unwashed will score poorly.

*Tips for scoring high in personal turnout*

- Make sure your shoes are clean and polished;
- Shirt, trousers and tie will set a good image;
- Ensure your clothes are ironed and not creased;
- Work on your personal hygiene and overall appearance. Make sure your nails are clean.
- Stand tall and be confident;
- Don't slouch in the interview chair.

## SOCIABILITY

This section assesses your ability to mix well with people. The Army want to know that you are socially confident and outgoing. It is also important that you have a good sense of humour. They want to know that you can fit in well with the Army way of life and that you have no problems with communal living.

When you join the Parachute Regiment you will be required to live in accommodation that comprises of other people. Some people find it very difficult to socialise with others and these are not the type of people the Army want to recruit, especially as Officers. They need people who will fit into the team spirit and whom have no problem with communicating with others. Those applicants who come across as quiet or shy will not score well in the area of sociability. At no point during selection should you be brash, abrasive or not a team player.

*Tips for scoring high in sociability*

> During the interviews provide examples of where you have mixed well with others. This may be through your current work position of with youth organisations such as the Scouts or Cadets etc;

> If you have played team sports then this will be an advantage;

> Tell the interviewer that you will have no problem with communal living. Communal living is living with other people. During your Officer Initial Training you will be required to live in a room with other Officers, so the Army want to know that you are comfortable with this;

> Smile and laugh where appropriate – a sense of humour is a must

but never be over bearing or over confident. Never 'back chat' or be disrespectful to the recruiting officers and staff.

## EMOTIONAL MATURITY AND STABILITY

The Army want to see that you are mature for your age and that you are even tempered and well balanced. This is especially important when applying to join as an Officer. They don't want people who are aggressive or who come across with a bad attitude. They want to see that you have coped well with the ups and downs of life so far and you may find that they ask you questions on any difficult areas of life that you have had to deal with. They want to know that you will adapt well to the change in lifestyle when you join the Army and that you can cope in highly stressful situations. The Army will also be looking for you to be mature for your age and that there are no signs of depression or anxiety. They will also be assessing your ability to cope well with unfamiliar surroundings and that you will not become homesick during training.

*Tips for scoring high in emotional maturity and stability*

> During the interviews and during discussions with the Armed Forces Careers Officer advisor try to provide examples of where you have dealt well with difficult situations in your life in a positive and mature manner;

> Try to be upbeat and positive about the future;

> Don't be overconfident or macho.

## DRIVE AND DETERMINATION TO SUCCEED

The Army want to know that you have a sense of purpose in your life. They will be looking for a pattern of achievement, either through school, university or at work, and for evidence that you are not easily deflected from your goals and aspirations. They want to see that you are a competitive person who is highly motivated to succeed. Perseverance is my favourite word. If I persevere, then I will be successful. Drive and determination are very similar to perseverance in that you have the ability to keep working hard and improving yourself until you achieve success.

Those applicants who show signs that they give up easily or have no goals aspirations will score poorly in the area of drive and determination to succeed.

*Tips for scoring high in drive and determination to succeed*

> Provide examples of where you have 'achieved'. This might be educational qualifications, courses that you have attended or even sporting achievements;

> Be positive about joining the Army and tell them that nothing is going to stop you from succeeding. If you don't pass this time then you will look for ways to improve for the next time you apply;

> Demonstrate that your ambition and sense of purpose is to join the Army and become a professional and competent Officer.

## PHYSICALLY ROBUST

The Army want to see that you engage in outdoor activities and that you have some experience in playing team sports. Being physically active is important and if you are strong and free from injuries and weakness then this will be an advantage during selection. If you are not involved in any form of team sports then I advise that you start straight away. As you can imagine, the Parachute Regiment rely heavily on team-work and team spirit. It is very easy to become involved in team sports as there are so many to choose from. Examples of team sports include football and rugby.

Those applicants who provide evidence that they are generally isolated individuals who spend too much time at home on the computer or watching TV will score lower than those who are physically active.

*Tips for scoring high in physical robustness*

• Be involved in competitive team sports;

• Be an active outdoor type person;

• Attend the gym and carry out light weight exercises and workouts.

## EXPERIENCE OF BEING SELF RELIANT

The Army want to know that you can handle the pressure of living away from home. If you have travelled or have been on camps where you have had to 'rough it' then this would be an advantage. Basically they want to know that you can look after yourself without the help of your parents or home comforts.

If you have no experience whatsoever of being self reliant then I advise that you take steps to improve your experience in this area. For example, there is nothing to stop you from going camping for the weekend or joining the Army Cadets where you will be able to gain experience of this important attribute.

### Tips for scoring high in being self reliant

> Provide examples of where you have been away from home for short or long periods of time;

> Tell the interviewer that you enjoy travelling and being away from home. Remember that it is important to provide examples of where you have already done this.

> Tell the interviewer that you are looking forward to leaving home to join the Parachute Regiment and face the challenges that it presents;

> Provide examples of where you have had to fend for yourself or where you have been away camping.

## REACTIONS TO SOCIAL DISCIPLINE

The Army want to see that you have a positive attitude towards authority. People in authority include the police, your parents, teachers and even your boss at work. When you join the Parachute Regiment you will initially be taking orders from Senior Officers and they want to know that you have no problem with authority. As you progress through your career and complete your Officer Initial Training, it will be you who is giving the orders.

There is a strong possibility that the interviewer will ask you questions that relate to your attitude to education and your teachers. At no point should you be negative about your teachers or about people whom are in positions of authority. If you are disrespectful or negative about these people then there is a strong possibility that the Army Selection Officers will take a dim view on your attitude and you won't be put forward to the AOSB briefing. For example, I have been aware of applicants who complain during the Army Interview that their teachers were rubbish at their job and that every-one in the class would always laugh at them. As you can imagine, those applicants do not progress any further during the selection process.

## Tips for scoring high in social discipline

> Try to provide examples of where you have carried out orders, either at work or at school;

> Tell the interviewer that you respect authority, providing you do of course, and that you see it as an important aspect of life. You do not have a problem with taking orders from anyone, even if they are the opposite sex to you.

## EXPERIENCE AND REACTION TO REGIMENT AND ROUTINE

When you join the Parachute Regiment you will initially lose much of your personal freedom. During your initial training there will be many restrictions placed upon you in terms of leave and your general freedom. You won't be given the time to do all of the things that you usually do whilst at home. Therefore, the Army want to see that you have the ability to cope with this added pressure and disciplined routine.

You must try to demonstrate during the selection process that you have already experienced some form of routine and that you are capable of following rules and regulations. This could simply be by having some form of disciplined routine at home, whereby you are required to clean the house and carry out the ironing for a few hours every week.

## Tips for scoring high in experience of and reaction to regimentation and routine

> Provide examples of where you have lost your personal freedom, either during your up-bringing, at school or during work. Maybe you have had to work unsociable hours or had to dedicate time and effort into your educational studies or degree course?

> Tell the interviewer that you fully understand that you will lose your personal freedom when you join the Parachute Regiment and that it won't be a problem for you.

> Implement some form of routine into your preparation strategy for joining the Paras. Set out your action plan early on and follow it rigidly.

## KNOWLEDGE AND EXPERIENCE OF ARMY/PARACHUTE REGIMENT LIFE

Having knowledge of Army/Parachute Regiment life can be achieved in a number of ways. If you have been a member of any youth organisations then this will be an obvious advantage. Youth organisations include the Scouts, Army Cadets, Air Training Corps or Sea Cadets etc. If a member of your family or a friend is a member of the Armed Forces then you can also gain knowledge through them, simply by asking them questions about their job and life within the Armed Forces. It is also important to gain knowledge of Army/Parachute Regiment life by reading your recruitment literature and visiting the Army website if you have access to the Internet.

Another fantastic way to gain invaluable knowledge of how the Army operates and its equipment is to grab yourself a copy of the book entitled 'The British Army: A Pocket Guide'. This book usually sells for approximately £5.99 and it fits easily into your pocket. Any spare moments you have during the day you can get the book out and start reading about vital facts that relate to the British Army and the Parachute Regiment.

### *Tips for scoring high in knowledge and experience of Army/ Parachute Regiment life*

> Speak to any friends or relatives who are members of the Armed Forces and ask them what it is like. Gain as much information as possible from the Armed Forces Careers Office staff and also through your recruitment literature;

> Find out as much as possible about the training you will undertake when you join the Parachute Regiment as an Officer;

> Consider visiting an Army establishment or museum. These are great places to learn about Army life.

> Consider joining a youth organisation such as the Scouts or cadets to gain some experience of a disciplined service.

## MOTIVATION TO JOIN THE PARACHUTE REGIMENT

The Army want to see that it is your own decision to join the Paras and that you haven't been pushed into it by friends or your family. They want to see that you have been pulled by the attractions of the Paras as opposed to being pushed into them. If you are successful in your application the Army will be investing a tremendous amount of time, energy and finances into your training and development. The last thing they want is that you decide it's not for you.

### Tips for scoring high in motivation to join the Parachute Regiment

> Always present a positive attitude towards joining when you visit the Armed Forces Careers Office and also whilst attending the POIC and the AOSB. This choice of career should be something that you considered very carefully about and you have been working very hard to make sure that you pass;

> Try to think about what attracts you to the Regiment and tell the interviewer during selection.

## PERSONAL CIRCUMSTANCES

The Army will want to know that you have the support of your family and/ or your partner. They also want to see that you are free from any detracting circumstances such as financial difficulties. If you are in financial difficulty then this could have a negative effect on your mental health during training. They will assess your personal circumstances during selection and also at the POIC and the AOSB interviews.

### Tips for scoring high in personal circumstances

> Speak to your parents and your partner (if applicable) about your choice of career. Ask them for their support;

> If they do not support you or they are concerned about you joining then I would recommend that you take them along to the careers office so that the Army Forces Careers Officer can talk to them about Army/Parachute Regiment life and answer any questions that they may have. It is imperative that you have their full support.

## EXPERIENCE OF LEADERSHIP AND MANAGEMENT

Because you are applying to join the Paras as an Officer, it would be wise to gain some experience as a leader or manager before you apply. The Army will ask you the question "What experience do you have so far as a leader of manager?" If you don't have any experience in these important areas then how do you know you'll make a good Parachute Regiment Officer?

There are many ways in which you can gain supervisory, leadership or managerial experience as follows:

> Ask your manager at work if you can shadow him/her for a week to see how they manage their staff and their responsibilities.

> Take charge of a sporting team.

> Arrange a charity event with a group of friends and volunteer to be the one who organises and arranges the event.

> Volunteer to be the captain of a sporting team.

It is important that you try to gain some form of managerial experience before you join.

During the next section of this guide I will provide you with some useful information as to how you will be assessed during the AOSB.

## THE AOSB SCORING CRITERIA

Before I go onto explain the scoring criteria, let us first of all take a look at some of the competencies required to successfully pass Army Officer Initial Training at Sandhurst.

### COMPETENCIES REQUIRED FOR SUCCESS DURING OFFICER INITIAL TRAINING

#### *Interpersonal Competencies*

| | |
|---|---|
| Communication | Communicates accurately and effectively, both orally and in writing. |
| Teamwork | Works willingly with others to achieve common goals. |
| Influence | Persuades others to follow a certain course of action. |

#### *Problem Solving Competencies*

| | |
|---|---|
| Appreciation | Comprehends, identifies, extracts and assimilates information from a range of sources, quickly and accurately. |

| Reasoning | Thinks logically, practically and coherently to produce a successful or reasonable solution, quickly and accurately. |
|---|---|
| Organisation | Determines priorities and allocates resources effectively and efficiently to a task(s). |
| Capacity | Holds and processes multiple inputs whilst maintaining task performance. |

## Character Competencies

| Decisiveness | Makes sound appropriate decisions within a timescale demanded by the situation. |
|---|---|
| Self-motivation | Demonstrates a high level of commitment and interest to tasks. |
| Self-analysis | Monitors and objectively analyses own performance |
| Integrity | Behaviour is guided by principles, morals and ethics appropriate to service life. Adheres to rules and regulations specific to the Army. |

Now that we understand some of the competencies that are required to pass Officer Initial Training, we can explore the assessable qualities required in order to successfully pass the Army Officer Main Board.

## Some of the competencies assessed during AOSB Main Board

| Competency | Descriptors |
|---|---|
| Oral and written communication | Delivery; effectiveness/understanding; listening. Is able to write in a clear, relevant and concise manner. |
| Teamwork | Can work with others to achieve a common goal or task; treatment of others; effort and determination. |
| Influence | Impact on others; directing; persuasiveness. |

| Problem Solving | Judgment/reasoning; flexibility; comprehension; capacity; decisiveness. |
| Confidence and Resilience | Self assurance; composure; perseverance; assertion. |

The Army Selecting Officers will use these and other competencies to assess your performance during the AOSB Main Board. It is therefore imperative that you score positively in every area. Here's an example of how you can score positively, and also negatively, in the assessable area of oral communication.

## ORAL COMMUNICATION

**Standard - Good**

**Delivery**
Forceful projection, clear delivery, concise and relevant.

**Effectiveness / Understanding**
Concise, succinct, articulate, lucid, easily understood, uses language/style appropriate to audience.

**Listening**
Listening to others' views attentively, asks patient questions to clarify.

**Standard - Acceptable**

**Delivery**
Expresses self clearly, good pace, good projection.

**Effectiveness / Understanding**
Coherent, understandable, covers all points, comprehensive brief, speaks fluently.

**Listening**
Listening to others' suggestions

**Standard – Requires development**

**Delivery**
Makes himself heard, projection varies, projection ok but drops, slight tendency to mumble, is quiet under pressure.

**Effectiveness / Understanding**
Covers most points, team didn't always understand, not concise lengthy briefs, inappropriate language – sense of occasion, rapid delivery, slight ponderous speech, disjointed brief, sometimes had to repeat brief.

**Listening**
Listens to major contributors in the group only.

**Standard** - Poor

**Delivery**
Mumbles, mutters, monotonous, voice does not carry, whispers, barely audible, tends to slur words.

**Effectiveness / Understanding**
Monosyllabic, wooden, rambles, meaningless chatter, verbose, garrulous, struggles forming sentences, couldn't understand what his/her point was.

**Listening**
Doesn't listen to others' views, talks over other and interrupts.

It is clear from the above sample standards that you need to be aiming for GOOD; therefore, you should structure your communication around these areas.

## WHEN ARE THE COMPETENCIES ASSESSED?

Each of the competencies are assessed during every stage and it is therefore important that you try to demonstrate them.

# CHAPTER 4
# THE ARMY CAREERS ADVISOR (ACA) INTERVIEW

During the Parachute Regiment Officer Selection process you will be required to sit interviews at the Armed Forces Careers Office (AFCO), the Potential Officer Insight Course (POIC) and also during your attendance at the Army Officer Selection Board (AOSB). Whilst the questions and tips contained within this section of the guide concentrate primarily on the ACA interview, they are also great preparation for the POIC and AOSB too.

The interview, which is held at your local Armed Forces Careers Office, will be undertaken by an Army Careers Advisor. The purpose of this interview is to 'filter' out those people who have the potential to become a Parachute Regiment Officer and those that don't. If you have the potential, then you will get put forward to attend the POIC and the AOSB briefing.

The duration of the initial ACA interview will very much depend on your responses to the questions. However, you can expect the interview to last for approximately 60 minutes. The questions that you will be assessed against during the initial interview will normally be taken from the following areas:

• The reasons why you want to join the Parachute Regiment and why you have chosen the Army over the Royal Navy and the Royal Air Force;

• Why you want to become a Parachute Regiment Officer and what skills, qualities and experiences you have that would help you to become a competent Officer.

• What area(s) of specialism you are most interested in, the reason for choosing them and the skills you have to match the role;

• What information you already know about the Army/Parachute Regiment its history, its lifestyle and training;

• Information relating to your hobbies and interests including sporting/team activities;

• Any personal responsibilities that you currently have at home, in your education or at work;

• Information about your family and your partner and what they think about you joining;

• Your educational qualifications;

• Information based around your initial application and CV;

• Your experience of work and education;

• Your emotional stability and your maturity;

• Your drive and determination to succeed;

• Experiences that you have already gained as a manager, leader or supervisor;

• Having a positive reaction to a disciplined environment and towards people in positions of authority.

Before I move on to a number of sample interview questions and responses I want to explain a little bit about interview technique and how you can come across in a positive manner during the interview.

During my career in the Fire Service I sat on many interview panels assessing people who wanted to become firefighters. As you can imagine there were some good applicants and there were also some poor ones. Let me explain the difference between a good applicant and a poor one.

## A GOOD APPLICANT

A good applicant is someone who has taken the time to prepare. They have researched both the organisation they are applying to join and also the role that they are being interviewed for. They may not know every detail about the organisation and the role but it will be clear that they have made an effort to find out important facts and information. They will be well presented at the interview and they will be confident, but not over confident. As soon as they walk into the interview room they will be polite and courteous and they will sit down in the interview chair only when invited to do so. Throughout the interview they will sit up right in the chair and communicate in a positive manner. If they do not know the answer to a question they will say so and they won't try and waffle. At the end of the interview they will ask positive questions about the job or the organisation before shaking hands and leaving.

## A POOR APPLICANT

A poor applicant could be any combination of the following. They will be late for the interview or even forget to turn up at all. They will have made little effort to dress smart and they will have carried out little or no preparation. When asked questions about the job or the organisation they will have little or no knowledge. Throughout the interview they will appear to be unenthusiastic about the whole process and will look as if they want the interview to be over as soon as possible. Whilst sat in the interview chair they will slouch and fidget. At the end of the interview they will try to ask clever questions that are intended to impress the panel.

I strongly advise that you try out a 'mock' interview before the real ACA interview. You'll be amazed at how much your confidence will improve. All you need to do is get your parents or a friend to sit down with you and ask you the interview questions that are contained within this guide. Try to answer them as if you were at the real interview. The more mock interviews you try the more confident you'll become.

## INTERVIEW TECHNIQUE

How you present yourself during the interview is important. Whilst assessing candidates for interviews I will not only assess their responses to the interview questions but I will also pay attention to the way they present themselves. A candidate could give excellent responses to the interview questions, but if they present themselves in a negative manner, then this can lose them valuable marks.

Take a look at the following diagrams which indicate both poor technique and good technique.

## POOR INTERVIEW TECHNIQUE

The candidate appears to be too relaxed and casual for an interview.

His elbow is resting on the corner of the chair which indicates an over confident attitude.

The candidate is wearing jeans and is too casually dressed for a formal interview.

The candidate's legs are crossed and his feet are not resting on the floor. This displays a relaxed and casual manner.

## GOOD INTERVIEW TECHNIQUE

The candidate is smiling and he portrays a confident, but not over confident manner.

The candidate is dressed wearing a smart suit. It is clear that he has made an effort in his presentation.

His hands are in a stable position which will prevent him from fidgeting. He could also place his hands palms facing downwards and resting on his knees.

He is sitting upright in the interview chair with his feet resting on the floor. He is not slouching and he portrays himself in a positive manner.

In the build up to your initial ACA interview practice a few 'mock' interviews. Look to improve your interview technique as well as working on your responses to the interview questions.

Now let's take a look at a number of sample interview questions. Please note that these questions are not guaranteed to be the exact ones you'll come up against at the real interview, but they are great starting point in your preparation. Use the sample responses that I have provided as a basis for your own preparation. Construct your answers on your own opinions and experiences.

## THE ARMED FORCES CAREERS OFFICE INTERVIEW FOR JOINING THE ARMY AS A PARCHUTE REGIMENT OFFICER

The Army will use a set marking sheet for your interviews and the questions will be based around a number of specific criteria. The questions will vary from interview to interview but the core elements are designed to assess whether you are suitable to join the Regiment as an Officer and progress onto the POIC and the AOSB. The following is a list of areas you may be asked questions on during your Army Careers Advisor interview and I would recommend that you use these as a basis for your preparation:

- The reasons why you want to join the Army and in particular the Parachute Regiment.
- The reasons why you want to become an Officer.
- The reasons why you have chosen your particular job, trade and Regiment.
- What information you already know about the Army, the Parachute Regiment and the lifestyle/training.
- Information about your hobbies and interests including sporting activities.
- Any personal responsibilities that you currently have at home, at college/ university or at work.
- Information about your family and what they think about you joining the Army. Do they support you?
- Information based around your initial application form.
- Your experience of work and education and whether or not you have had any responsibility at home or work.
- Any positions of authority you have held either at school, college, university, work or otherwise.
- Your emotional stability and your maturity.
- Your drive and determination to succeed.
- Any experience you have of working as part of a team.
- Your attitude towards physical exercise and team sports.
- Having a positive reaction to the disciplined environment.
- Your knowledge of life within the Army and the Parachute Regiment.

Over the next few pages I have provided you with a number of sample interview questions and responses. These will act as a good basis for your preparation. However, it is important to point out at this stage the responses you provide during the interview should be based solely on your own experiences and opinions.

## SAMPLE INTERVIEW QUESTION NUMBER 1

### Why do you want to join the Army?

This is an almost guaranteed question during your ACA interview so there should be no reason why you can't answer it in a positive manner. Try to display motivation when answering questions of this nature. The Army is looking for people who want to become a professional member of their team and who understand the Army way of life. By studying your Army recruitment literature and the Army website you will understand what service life is all about. You want to be an Officer of the British Army and you are attracted to what it has to offer. If you have been pushed into joining by your family then you shouldn't be applying.

## SAMPLE RESPONSE TO INTERVIEW QUESTION NUMBER 1

### Why do you want to join the Army?

"I have wanted to join the Army, and in particular the Parachute Regiment for a number of years now and feel that I have now reached a part of my life where I am ready to commit to the service. Having studied the Army recruitment literature and visited the Army website, I am impressed by the professionalism and standards the service sets.

I would like a career that is fulfilling, challenging and rewarding and I believe that the Army would provide all of these. I enjoy keeping physically fit and active and believe that given the right training I would make a great Officer within the Regiment.

The fact that I would be improving my education and receiving highly professional training as an Officer is just another example of why I want to join the Regiment. I have seriously considered the implications that joining the Army would have on both my personal life and social life and discussed these with my family. They have given me their full support and commitment in helping me to achieve my goal of joining the Army as an Officer.'

## SAMPLE INTERVIEW QUESTION NUMBER 2

*What does your family think of you wanting to join the Army?*

Again, you are likely to be asked a question surrounding your family background and what they think about you wanting to join the Army. It is important that your family support you in your decision.

If they have any doubts about you joining the service then you may wish to consider taking them along to the AFCO so they can ask any questions or raise any concerns that they may have. When answering questions such as this it is important that you are honest and tell the truth. If your family has any concerns, share them with the careers officer, who will then be able to advise you on the best way for your family/partner to overcome any fears they may have.

### SAMPLE RESPONSE TO INTERVIEW QUESTION NUMBER 2

*What does your family think of you wanting to join the Army?*

*'I have discussed the issue with them in depth and also shown them all of the Army recruitment literature to try to dampen any fears that they may have. They were initially concerned about me joining but they gave me their full support after I told them everything I know about the Officer Initial Training I will go through and the conditions I will serve under in the Parachute Regiment. They are aware that the Army has a formidable reputation and this has helped them to further understand why I want to join. They have seen how enthusiastic I am about wanting to join the Paras and know that it will be great for me. I have also discussed the issue with my partner and he/she is extremely supportive.*

## SAMPLE INTERVIEW QUESTION NUMBER 3

*How do you think you will cope with Army life in relation to the discipline and being part of a military organisation?*

When you join the Paras you will be joining a military organisation that has set procedures, standards and discipline codes. To some people this will come as a shock and the Army wants to know that you are prepared for this change in lifestyle. They are investing time, effort and resources into your training so they want to know that you can cope with their way of life. As you probably already know, the Parachute Regiment puts its men through extreme physical and mental training and you need to be 100% sure you can rise to the challenge that lies ahead.

When answering this type of question you need to demonstrate both your awareness of what Army life involves and also your positive attitude towards the disciplined environment. Study the recruitment literature and visit the Army website to get a feel for the type of training you will be going through.

## SAMPLE RESPONSE TO INTERVIEW QUESTION NUMBER 3

*How do you think you will cope with Army life in relation to the discipline and being part of a military organisation?*

'Having read the information available to me about the Army way of life I think I would cope very well. I know that I will find it difficult at times but believe I have both the maturity and stability to succeed and become a competent and professional Officer in the Parachute Regiment. The very nature of the Parachute Regiment means that it requires a highly disciplined and focused workforce. Without that discipline things can go wrong. If I am successful and do not carry out my duties professionally then I could endanger somebody's life. I understand why discipline is required and believe I would cope with it well. I understand that being in the Army isn't a 9-5 job, but instead you must take on tasks whenever required.

In order to prepare for the training I have already integrated routine and self discipline into my life. For example, I have been getting up at 6am every weekday morning to go running and I have started carrying out daily household tasks such as washing, cleaning and ironing. At the start of my preparation for joining the Army I made myself an action plan that would focus my mind on what I needed to do in order to improve.'

## SAMPLE INTERVIEW QUESTION NUMBER 4

*How do you think you will cope with being away from home and losing your personal freedom?*

This type of question is one that needs to be answered positively. There is only one correct answer to this question and you need to demonstrate that you have considered the consequences of leaving home and are fully aware of what is involved. If you have any experience of being away from home then you should state this in your response. Try to think of occasions when you have been away for periods of time and tell them that it wasn't an issue.

Have you ever been a part of any youth organisations? If you have then this will undoubtedly go in your favour. Giving an example is far better than just saying you will be able to cope.

## SAMPLE RESPONSE INTERVIEW QUESTION NUMBER 4

*How do you think you will cope with being away from home and losing your personal freedom?*

'Having already had experience of being away from home, I believe I would cope extremely well. Whilst serving with the Scouts a few years ago I was introduced to the Army way of life and fully understand what it is like to be away from home. I actually enjoy being away from home and I can't wait to get started if I am successful during Officer selection. I understand, however, that the training is difficult and intense and I am fully prepared for this. I am confident that I will cope with the change in lifestyle very well and I am looking forward to the challenge if I am accepted.'

## SAMPLE INTERVIEW QUESTION NUMBER 5

*Are you involved in any sporting activities and how do you keep yourself fit?*

When answering questions based around your own physical fitness you need to be honest but bear in mind the following points:

The standard of physical fitness required to serve in the Parachute Regiment is high. As an Officer in the Regiment you must lead by example and that means being at peak physical fitness. The bleep test standard set at AOSB is only 10.2. If you can't reach that level then you need your butt kicking! Personally, I recommend you can reach level 14 before you attend POIC and AOSB. Level 14 is tough to reach, but with a bit of hard work it is achievable.

The Parachute Regiment pride themselves on their ability to work as an effective team unit. Those people who engage in active team sports are more likely to be competent team members. If you play a team sport then this will be a good thing to tell them. If you don't then it may be a good idea to go and join one!

Regardless of the above points, remember that if you don't do any physical activity whatsoever then you will score low in this area. Make sure you partake in some form of physical activity. If you don't already have a copy of the bleep test you can obtain one from www.how2become.co.uk.

## SAMPLE RESPONSE TO INTERVIEW QUESTION NUMBER 5

*Are you involved in any sporting activities and how do you keep yourself fit?*

'Yes I am. I currently Captain the local rugby team and have done for some years now. I am very passionate about my fitness levels and spend at least 30 minutes every day doing either swimming, running or rugby training. In the buildup to preparing for selection I have also started working on my bleep level fitness and can now reach level 14 comfortably.  Maintaining a high level of fitness is something I enjoy and it is also great for my mental attitude. I am fully aware that during the Officer Initial Training course I will be pushed to my limits so I need to be prepared for that. I believe the fact that I play team sports will help me get through my training.

I enjoy leading the rugby team because when we are being beaten by another team I rise to the challenge and motivate the team to work towards winning. After the game we all meet in the club bar for a drink and a chat about the game. Keeping fit is important to me and something that I want to continue doing throughout my career if I am successful in joining the Parachute Regiment. I also feel it is important to act as a role model for the men whom are under your command. If I expect my men to be physically fit then I need to be too'

## SAMPLE INTERVIEW QUESTION NUMBER 6

*How do you think you will fit into a team environment?*

Before you apply to join the Parachute Regiment it is essential you have experience of working in a team. Maybe you have experience of working in a sporting team or need to work as a team in your current job? Try to think of examples where you have already been working in a team environment and if you can provide an example where the team achieved something then even better. Structure your answer around your own experiences and also around your knowledge of the fact that the Army needs to work as an effective team unit in order for it to complete its tasks both safely and on time. The key to responding to this question effectively is to provide the interviewer with 'evidence' of where you have already worked successfully as part of a team.

## SAMPLE RESPONSE TO INTERVIEW QUESTION NUMBER 6

### *How do you think you will fit into a team environment?*

*'I have experience of both working in a team and leading one. I Captain and play for a local rugby team and fully understand how important it is for everybody to get together in order to win our games. For any team task to be achieved a team must focus on the end goal and forget about egos or differences within the team. The real test for any team is when things are not going right. It is then that a team must really pull together, communicate well, support each other and create positive action in order to achieve the objective. I understand that the Parachute regiment needs to work together effectively as a team to get the right result. If the team doesn't perform then people's lives can be put at risk. Being an effective part of the team also means that I would have to train hard and keep up my competency levels, which I believe I would do well.*

*With my experience of team sports and having the ability to pull a team together when the chips are down, I think I would be a great asset to the Army team.'*

## SAMPLE INTERVIEW QUESTION NUMBER 7

### *What do you do in your spare time?*

With questions of this nature the Army Careers Advisor is looking to see if you use your leisure time wisely. Your response will tell them a lot about your attitude and motivation. We all know that some people spend their spare time doing nothing, watching TV or spending hours on Facebook. When you join the Parachute Regiment as an Officer you won't have much time to sit around and do nothing. The Army will want to hear that you are active and doing worthwhile things during your spare time. For example, if you are involved in any sports, outdoor activities or are part of any youth organisation such as the Army Cadets, then these are good things to tell them. You may also be involved in voluntary work or charity work and once again these will work in your favour if mentioned at interview.

If you currently do very little with your spare time then now is a good time to make a lifestyle change. Embark on a fitness routine or join an activity club or organisation.

## SAMPLE RESPONSE TO INTERVIEW QUESTION NUMBER 7

### What do you do in your spare time?

'During my spare time I like to keep active, both physically and mentally. I enjoy visiting the gym five times a week and I have a structured workout that I try to vary every three months to keep my interest levels up. I'm also currently doing a part-time study course in Art, which is one of my hobbies. I'm also a member of the local Army Cadets, which is an evening's commitment every week and the occasional weekend.

I also know when it is time to relax and usually do this by either listening to music or playing snooker with my friends, but overall I'm quite an active person. I certainly don't like sitting around doing nothing. I understand that if I'm successful at joining the Army there will be plenty of things to do in the evenings to keep me occupied such as the gym, study time and preparing for the next days training.

## SAMPLE INTERVIEW QUESTION NUMBER 8

### Can you tell us about any personal achievements you have experienced during your life so far?

Having achieved something in your life demonstrates that you have the ability to see things through to the end. It also shows that you are motivated and determined to succeed. This is especially true when applying to become an Officer in the Parachute Regiment. The Army wants to see evidence that you can achieve, as there is a greater chance of you completing the Officer Initial Training course at Sandhurst if you have a history of this. Try to think of examples where you have succeeded or achieved something relevant in your life. Some good examples of achievements are as follows:

• Duke of Edinburgh's Award;

• A-levels, degrees or educational qualifications;

- Team or individual sports awards/trophies/medals;

- Raising money for charity.

Obviously you will have your own achievements that you will want to add in your response.

## SAMPLE RESPONSE TO INTERVIEW QUESTION NUMBER 8

*Can you tell us about any personal achievements you have experienced during your life so far?*

'So far in my life I have managed to achieve a number of things that I am proud of. To begin with, I recently worked hard to achieve my 'A' level results, which enabled me to go on to university to study for my degree. Without these grades I would not have been able to do that.

About a year ago the football team that I play in won the league trophy for the second year running, which is another one of my more recent achievements. I was particularly pleased because I was the Captain of the team and played a large part in its organisation and development.

However, my most memorable achievement to date is managing to raise £4,000 for a local charity. I worked hard and ran a marathon in order to raise the money. I was particularly proud of this achievement because It meant the charity I ran for were able to purchase some important items of equipment that could be used to treat some of their patients.'

## SAMPLE INTERVIEW QUESTION NUMBER 9

*What are your strengths?*

This is a common interview question, which is relatively easy to answer. The problem with it is that many people use the same response. It is quite an easy thing to tell the interviewer that you are dedicated and the right person for the job. However, it is a different thing backing it up with evidence!

If you are asked this type of question make sure you are positive during your response and show that you actually mean what you are saying. Then, back your answer up with examples of when you have demonstrated a strength that you say you have. For example, if you tell the panel that you are a motivated person, back it up with an event in your life where you achieved something through sheer motivation and determination.

SAMPLE RESPONSE TO INTERVIEW QUESTION NUMBER 9

## What are your strengths?

*'To begin with I am a determined person who likes to see things through to the end. For example, I recently ran a marathon for charity. I'd never done this kind of thing before and found it very hard work, but I made sure I completed the task. Another strength of mine is that I'm always looking for ways to improve myself. As an example, whilst preparing for Officer selection I have embarked on a Diploma in Management Studies through the Open University to give me an insight into management and leadership.*

*Finally, I would say that one of my biggest strengths is that I'm a great team player. I really enjoy working in a team environment and achieving things through a collaborative approach. For example, I play in a local rugby team and we recently won the league trophy for the first time since the club was established some 50 years ago.'*

## SAMPLE INTERVIEW QUESTION NUMBER 10

## What is your biggest weakness?

Now there's a question! If we were all totally honest with ourselves we could probably write a whole list of weaknesses. Now, I wouldn't advise that you reel off a whole list of weaknesses in your interview, as you could do yourself a lot of harm. Conversely, those people who say that they don't have any weaknesses are probably not telling the truth.

If you are asked a question of this nature then it is important that you give at least one weakness. The trick here is to make the weakness sound like a strength. For example, a person may say that one of their weaknesses is that their own personal standards are too high sometimes and they expect this of others. Or another one is that a person doesn't know when to relax. They are always on the go achieving and making things happen when they should take more time out to relax and recuperate.

SAMPLE RESPONSE TO INTERVIEW QUESTION NUMBER 10

## What is your biggest weakness?

*'That's a difficult question but I know that I do have a particular weakness. The standards that I always set myself are quite high and unfortunately I*

*get frustrated when other peoples aren't. For example, I am never late for anything and believe that punctuality is really important. However, if I'm left waiting for other people who are late I usually have to say something to them when they finally arrive, which doesn't always go down too well.'*

## SAMPLE INTERVIEW QUESTION NUMBER 11

*Can you tell me why you want to become an Officer?*

Once again, an almost guaranteed question so make sure you have prepared for it fully. You must have valid reasons why you want to become an Officer in the Parachute Regiment. This job is entirely different to being a regular soldier. You will have far more responsibilities and the training that you will undergo will be extremely challenging, both mentally and physically. Here are a few positive reasons for wanting to become an Officer:

*"An opportunity to become an elite Officer in the Parachute Regiment is an opportunity to be the best that I can be."*

*"I believe that I have the potential to become an exceptional Officer and I don't want to waste my potential."*

*"I want to become an Officer simply because I believe I have the skills and attributes to lead, inspire and develop people. If I am not in a leadership position then I believe those skills and attributes will be wasted."*

*"I am a confident, professional and enthusiastic person who believes that everyone should be given the opportunity to be there best. As an Officer I would have the chance to make a difference and I would thrive in a position that could help the Regiment to achieve its organisational goals and objectives."*

*"In any organisation that I have worked in so far, I have always held a keen interest in the development of staff and the development of the company as a whole. The experiences that I have gained in life so far and prepared me to become an Officer in the Parachute Regiment and I believe that I could be a excellent member of the Regiments leadership team."*

## SAMPLE INTERVIEW QUESTION NUMBER 12

*What qualities do you think you need to be a good team player?*

The Parachute Regiment needs effective and competent team players.

It is important that you already have some experience of working in a team environment. Because you are applying to become an Officer it is also beneficial to have evidence of where you have led or managed a team of people too. Try to think of examples where you have already successfully contributed to a team task either at work or during your education and also where you have led a team. There are many different qualities required to work as an effective team player. Here are just a few:

• Enthusiastic;

• A good communicator;

• Motivated;

• Supportive of the other team members;

• Providing other team members with encouragement;

• Determined to complete the task;

• Professional and competent;

• Always focused on the wider team objective;

• Focused on the end goal;

• A willingness to develop and improve;

• Being able to adapt to changing circumstances.

Now take a look at the following sample response to this question.

SAMPLE RESPONSE TO INTERVIEW QUESTION NUMBER 12

*What qualities do you think you need to be a good team player?*

'First of all I believe a team player must be focused purely on the task that the team is trying to achieve. You must always be professional and support-ive of the other team members. For example, if one of the team members is struggling then you should try to help them and support them with their role within the team. It is important as a team player to listen to the brief or details of the task and to communicate properly with everyone else in the team. You must always put the needs of the team before your own and be totally committed to completing the task in hand. In relation to being an Officer then it is your responsibility to focus, motivate and lead your team towards to goals and missions of the Army."

## SAMPLE INTERVIEW QUESTION NUMBER 13

*What contact have you had with the Army and the Parachute Regiment during your application and what have you done to find out about Army life?*

Those applicants who are serious about a career in the Army/Parachute Regiment will have gone out of their way to find out about the service and what it involves. The Army Careers Advisor will want to see evidence that you have taken steps to speak to people who are already serving and that you have researched the organisation effectively. It is important that you are 100% committed to joining and that you are fully aware of the challenge that lies ahead of you. The following is a sample response to this question.

### SAMPLE RESPONSE TO INTERVIEW QUESTION NUMBER 13

*What contact have you had with the Army and the Parachute Regiment during your application and what have you done to find out about Army life?*

'*During my preparation I have carried out lots of research into the Army and the Parachute Regiment so that I am fully aware of the challenge that lies ahead of me. To begin with I have studied my recruitment literature in depth and I have also spent plenty of time browsing the Army recruitment website. I have also obtained a copy of the British Army Pocket Guide which has taught me lots about the service, the Regiments and the equipment. More recently I spent a couple of hours at my local Army establishment where I managed to speak to serving officers about their role and the job. I found this an invaluable insight. All of this research and reading has made me more excited about joining. I cannot wait to get started if I am successful.*'

## SAMPLE INTERVIEW QUESTION NUMBER 14

*What are the values of the British Army?*

During an earlier stage of this guide I made reference to the Army values. Every soldier and Officer is expected to abide by these important values and therefore it is not unreasonable for the Army to expect you to know them when you apply. You are likely to be asked a question that relates to the values during the ACA interview so make sure you know them and what each one of them means. Here is a sample response to this question.

## SAMPLE RESPONSE TO INTERVIEW QUESTION NUMBER 14

### *What are the values of the British Army?*

'The values of the British Army are a selfless commitment, courage, discipline, integrity, loyalty and respect for others. It is important to be strong and aggressive in battle but to also behave properly and demonstrate self control at all times. Army soldiers and officers have to be aggressive and strong in battle, yet behave properly and show self-control all of the time. Being courageous means facing up to danger and doing what is right at all times. Discipline means having the ability to maintain constant high standards, so that others can rely on you. Integrity means earning the respect and trust of your work colleagues. Loyalty is being faithful to your work colleagues and to your duty and having respect for others mean treating everybody with respect and dignity at all times.'

## SAMPLE INTERVIEW QUESTION NUMBER 15

### *What are you currently doing in order to prepare for Officer training?*

Whilst this question should be generally easy to answer, it does end up throwing many applicants. Most people who apply to join the Army will do little or no preparation for Officer Initial Training until they have received confirmation that they have passed the AOSB. However, if you can show the Army Careers Advisor that you are already preparing for training then this will impress them. Here is a sample response to assist you.

## SAMPLE RESPONSE TO INTERVIEW QUESTION NUMBER 15

### *What are you currently doing in order to prepare for Officer training?*

'Although I haven't passed the AOSB yet, I have been preparing thoroughly for my training. To begin with I have created a timetable of preparation which makes sure I work on my weak areas and my overall fitness. Every weekday I am up at 6am and I embark on a 4 mile run. This is so that I can get used to the early starts and so that I can improve my fitness levels. Half way round my run I always make sure I stop and carry out 50 press ups and 50 sit ups using the correct technique. When I get home from work I then sit down for an hour and work on my knowledge of the Army and the Parachute Regiment. Every other day I work on my aptitude test ability and I make sure I read a good quality newspaper so that I am up to date with Army operations and the more important current affairs issues. I have also been working hard on my ability to carry out speed, distance and time calculations. I have also obtained a management book that has given me an insight into how to be a good manager and leader. Finally, I have been working on my household skills and responsibilities such as ironing and cleaning.'

## SAMPLE INTERVIEW QUESTION NUMBER 16

### *Can you tell me what Officer Initial Training consists of?*

Before you attend your interview you must find out details about your initial training at Sandhurst. This information is available through the Army website at **www.army.mod.uk.**

## FURTHER ACA INTERVIEW QUESTIONS TO PREPARE FOR

- What do you think about your educational exam results? We're they what you expected?
- Where is the Army operating in the World right now?
- What parts of Officer Initial Training do you expect to find the hardest?
- What are you currently doing to improve on your weak areas?
- Why do you want to join the Parachute Regiment?
- What is the main role of the Parachute Regiment and where are they operating right now?
- What are the qualities of an Army Officer?
- What is the role of a Parachute Regiment Officer?

## INTERVIEW TIPS FOR THE ACA INTERVIEW

> When you walk into the interview room stand up straight with your shoulders back. Project an image of confidence;

> Don't sit down in the interview chair until invited to do so;

> Sit with your hands resting on your knees, palms downwards. It is OK to use your hands expressively but don't overdo it;

> Don't slouch in the chair;

> Speak up and be positive;

> Smile, be happy and have a sense of humour;

> Dress in a smart suit, shirt and tie and take a pride in your appearance. If you don't have a suit make sure you wear a shirt and tie at the very least.

> Make sure your shoes are shiny and clean. Do not wear jeans and trainers.

> Improve your personal administration. By this I mean your personal hygiene and cleanliness. Make sure you have washed and your hands and nails are clean.

> Make sure you have researched both the Army life and your chosen career/careers. This is very important.

> During the interview do not be negative or disrespectful towards your teachers, parents or people in positions of authority. Remember that you are applying to join a disciplined service.

> Go the extra mile and learn about the Parachute Regiments. When the panel asks you 'What can you tell us about the Parachute Regiment?' you will be able to demonstrate that you have made an effort to look into their history as well as their modern day activities;

> Be respectful and courteous towards the interview panel. At the end of your response to each question finish off with either 'Sir' or 'Ma'am' or as otherwise instructed.

> Ask positive questions at the end of the interview. Try not to ask questions such as "How much leave will I get?" or "How often do I get paid?"

> If you are unsure about a question don't waffle. If you do not know the answer then it is OK to say so. Move on to the next question and put it behind you.

> Finally, believe in yourself and be confident. A positive attitude will bring positive results!

# CHAPTER 5

# THE LEADERLESS TASK AND THE COMMAND TASK THAT FORM PART OF THE ARMY OFFICER SELECTION BOARD (AOSB)

## THE LEADERLESS TASK AND THE COMMAND TASK

During the Army Officer Selection Board you will be required to undertake both an outdoor Leaderless task and a Command task. Both tasks involve the solution of a 'practical' problem over an 'obstacle course'. In the Leaderless task there is no appointed leader, whereas in the Command task each candidate takes their turn as leader and must direct the rest of the group.

Let's now take a look at how you can achieve higher marks in each of the tasks.

# THE OUTDOOR LEADERLESS TASK

As the name suggests, this task is performed without a designated leader. The purpose of the assessment is to see how effective you are at working as part of a team and also to identify those people who have leadership potential. Those people who do have leadership potential will naturally come to the front and move the completion of the task forward.

As part of your group you will be provided with a task that must be completed within a set piece of time. The task might be a requirement for your group to move an object from point A to B, with certain restrictions in place, such as avoiding an area of floor space or only using specific items of equipment. Whatever the task/brief, it is important that you work effectively as a team member and try to come up with solutions to the problem.

Before I provide you with a number of tips to help you score higher during the leaderless task, let's take a look at a number of key areas that are essential to the smooth running of any task.

## *Component 1 – Time*
It is important that any team working towards a common goal is aware of the time constraints. Make sure everyone is aware of the time and keep checking it regularly if the facility exists.

## *Component 2 – Plan*
Every team that is working towards a common goal should have a plan in place. If you don't have a plan, how are you going to achieve the task in hand? The way to compile a successful plan is to ask the team if they have any ideas on how the task could be achieved.

## *Component 3 – Communication*
This is probably the most important component of any team task. Communication means talking to, and listening to, the other members of the team. Get this part wrong and the task is guaranteed to fail.

## *Component 4 – Allocation of tasks*
Everybody in the team will have different 'strengths'. You should try to find out who is good at what, and then allocate tasks accordingly.

## Component 5 – Support

It is the duty of every team member to support the other members of the team.

## Component 6 – URGENCY!

Regardless of how long you have to complete the task, urgency is a must.

Now let's take a look at a number of tips that will help you to pass the Leaderless task.

**TIP 1** – Although you should not 'take over' the task, you should at every opportunity attempt to demonstrate leadership 'potential'. This can be achieved in a number of ways. Once the brief has been provided, be the first to speak out:

*"OK everyone, shall we all form a plan in order to achieve the task in the most effective way possible? Does anyone have any suggestions as to how we can tackle this?"*

**TIP 2** – I recommend that you use the words 'plan' and 'time' during the leaderless task and the command task. These two components are the cornerstone of effective teamwork.

**TIP 3** – Be supportive of other team members and shout words of encouragement:

*"This is great team work everyone, let's keep going!"*

**TIP 4** – If the facility exists, keep an eye on the time.

**TIP 5** – Suggest allocating tasks to people who have skills in certain areas. For example, if there are any knots that need to be tied, ask if there's anyone in the team who is competent in this area.

**TIP 6** – Keep going, even if things start to go wrong and time is running out. Remember to always act with a sense of urgency!

**TIP 7** – Be active and get involved.

## THE OUTDDOR COMMAND TASK

The command task is different to the leaderless task in the fact that everyone in the group is required to take charge of an exercise/task.

You will be provided with a brief and you will then have a short period of time to brief the rest of your team and complete the required task. As you can imagine, the command task is harder than the leaderless task, simply because the spotlight is on you. It is crucial that you listen to the brief that will be provided by the Lead Officer. Once you have the brief, you will then need to explain your plan to the rest of the group, allocate tasks and generally co-ordinate proceedings.

### Briefing the team

Once you have received the brief from the Lead Officer you will have a short period of time to come up with a plan in order to achieve the task. Here is an excellent format to follow when briefing any team in a command situation:

### SMEAC

**Situation** – explain what the situation is.

*"OK, gather around team and pay attention whilst I explain the situation. Our task today is to… "*

**Mission** – once you have explained the situation, tell the team what the mission is.

*"Our mission is to…"*

**Execution** – tell your team how you are going to achieve the task including the allocation of tasks (plan).

*"We will achieve the task by carrying out XYZ."*

**Asking questions** – ask your team if anyone has any questions.

*"Is the brief clear team? Does anyone have any questions?"*

**Check for understanding** – check to see that your team fully understands what is expected from them.

*"Is everyone clear of the team task and their role within the team?"*

I have used SMEAC many times in the past during training exercises and also during firefighting operations. It provides a degree of organisation to any team and I would recommend that you learn it and use it during the command task when you are the person in charge.

Here's a list of tips to help you score higher during the command task exercise.

**TIP 1** – When you are not the person in charge, be an effective team leader. Help out as much as possible and get stuck in. You are assessed just as much on your ability to work with others as you are a leader. You may also wish to shout words of encouragement to the other members of the team.

*"Let's keep going everyone, we're doing a great job here."*

**TIP 2** – When you are the allocated person in charge, take control of your team

*"OK everyone, gather around and pay attention to the following brief..."*

**TIP 3** – Be supportive of your team members and get involved.

**TIP 4** – When briefing the team, consider using SMEAC.

**TIP 5** – If things start to go wrong, do not panic. Remain clam and in control. Keep going until the end and try your absolute hardest to complete the task. At the end of the task, whether it has been successful or not, thank your team for their efforts.

**TIP 6** – Keep an eye on safety. You are the person in charge and therefore responsible for safety.

# CHAPTER 6
# PREPARING FOR THE PLANNING EXERCISE

## PLANNING EXERCISE

You will most probably find this element of the AOSB the toughest. Before we look at how you can prepare effectively, here's an explanation as to what is involved.

## INDIVIDUAL STUDY TIME

Each person will be provided with a copy of the brief/setting. You will then have one hour to sit in silence, read the scenario and come up with a solution to the problem. It is important that you read everything carefully. Do not miss out any of the scenario as this could hinder you during the group discussion phase and questioning by the assessors. If you miss out anything, the assessors will pick up on it.

## GROUP DISCUSSION

Once the hour is complete you will then have a period of time to discuss the scenario, and how you intend to approach it, with the other candidates in your group. During this stage make sure you are vocal and active in the construction of the agreed plan – this is VERY important. Do not be afraid to make suggestions and if you have the confidence in your own plan, try and influence the other members of the group. Pay attention at all times, be involved and never dismiss someone's suggestions directly out of hand.

It is crucial that you are competent in the use of Speed, Distance and Time before you attend the AOSB. My advice is simple:

> Practice SDT questions everyday in the build up to the AOSB. You can obtain free SDT questions at the website:
**www.ArmyOfficerSelectionBoard.co.uk.**

> You should also practice SDT questions by having someone fire questions at you. This is a lot harder than working them out with a pen and paper!

Finally, be competent in the use of the 24 hour clock. The assessing officer's will expect you to use it when answering their questions.

## TOP TIPS FOR SCORING HIGH DURING THE PLANNING EXERCISE

- Demonstrate strength of character

- Don't give in, even if things are going wrong

- Support your decision and consider all eventualities

- Improve general arithmetic and be competent in the use of speed, distance and time (SDT)

- Be able to calculate SDT questions in your head, as well as being able to write them down. You can practice by getting a member of your family to ask you a series of SDT questions. This is great practice as you will be under pressure to answer the questions without the use of a calculator, pen and paper.

- Keep an eye on the time. You need to come up with a solution to the problem.

- Be alert and quick to respond to questions.

- Never lie when answering questions from the assessors, they will see straight through it. If you do not know the answer to a question, then just say so.

- Always remain calm. The questioning at the end of the exercise is designed to be tough and assess how well you cope under pressure.

## SPEED, DISTANCE AND TIME

Accuracy and agility in speed, distance, and time calculations will help you perform well during the Army Officer Selection process. The following information will assist you in understanding how to tackle these types of question.

When trying to solve these problems it is important to consider three variables: speed, distance and time. Try not to get too worried as two of these variables will always be known. The easiest way to solve these equations is to use the following formulas:

$$\text{Speed} = \frac{\text{Distance}}{\text{Time}}$$

$$\text{Distance} = \text{Speed} \times \text{Time}$$

$$\text{Time} = \frac{\text{Distance}}{\text{Speed}}$$

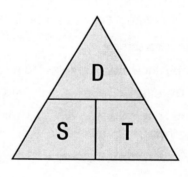

The triangular diagram above is ideal for helping you to remember the formula. Simply place your finger over the variable you are trying to discover, you will then see the equation required.

For example if you wanted to obtain the time, placing your finger on 'T' would show that you would need to *divide* distance (D) by speed (S).

Let's now work through some examples:

**1.** A train travels 60 miles in 3 hours. What is the train's speed?

> *Formula: Speed = distance ÷ time*
>
> Speed = 60 ÷ 3 = 20 mph

**2.** A car is travelling at 30 mph for 70 minutes. What is the distance travelled?

With this problem it is important to remember to work in minutes!

> So, 30 mph = 0.5 miles per minute (30 ÷ 60)

> 70 (minutes) × 0.5 = 35 miles

You can use the formula but you need to convert the minutes into hours and remember that 0.1 = 1/10 of 60 minutes:

> *Formula: Distance = speed × time*

> Distance = 30 × 1.1666r (1 hour 10 mins) = 35

**3.** A tank is driving at 48 mph over 60 miles. How long was it driving for?

> *Formula: Time = distance ÷ speed*

> Time = 60 ÷ 48 = 1 hour 15 minutes

Take these steps

I.   You know that 48 mph = 48 miles in 60 minutes.

II.   The difference between 60 and 48 is 12, which is ¼ of 48.

III. You can then take ¼ of 60, which gives 15 minutes, and add that to 60 minutes = 75 minutes.

IV. Then convert to hours = 1 hour 15 minutes for the answer!

OR

Take these steps

I.   You know that 48 mph = 0.8 miles per minute.

II.   60 ÷ 0.8 = 75 minutes.

III. Convert into hours = 1 hour 15 minutes.

Once you understand how to calculate speed, distance and time, take your time to work through the 30 sample test questions that follow.

In order to obtain further Speed, Distance and Time questions, and also try 8 planning exercises, please go to:

**www.ArmyOfficerAOSB.co.uk**

## SAMPLE SPEED, DISTANCE AND TIME TEST QUESTIONS

(Give all distances and speeds in whole numbers)

### Question 1

You are travelling at 28mph for 75 minutes. How far do you travel?

**Answer** ☐

### Question 2

You travel 15 miles in half an hour. What speed are you travelling at?

**Answer** ☐

### Question 3

You travel 33 miles at a constant speed of 55mph. How long are you travelling for?

**Answer** ☐

### Question 4

You are travelling at 75 mph for 1 and half hours. How far do you travel?

**Answer** ☐

### Question 5

You travel 61 miles in 1 hour and 5 minutes. What speed are you travelling at?

**Answer** ☐

### Question 6

You travel 90 miles at a constant speed of 30 mph. How long are you travelling for?

**Answer** ☐

### Question 7

You are travelling at 70mph for 125 minutes. How far do you travel?

**Answer** ☐

## Question 8

You travel 2.5 miles in 5 minutes. What speed are you travelling at?

**Answer**

## Question 9

You travel 75 miles at a constant speed of 45mph. How long are you travelling for?

**Answer**

## Question 10

You are travelling at 59 mph for quarter of an hour. How far do you travel?

**Answer**

## Question 11

You travel 325 miles in 4 hours and 6 minutes. What speed are you travelling at?

**Answer**

## Question 12

You travel 38 miles at 45 mph. How long are you travelling for?

**Answer**

## Question 13

You are travelling at 80 mph for 15 minutes. How far do you travel?

**Answer**

## Question 14

You travel 63 miles in 56 minutes. What speed are you travelling at?

**Answer**

## Question 15

You travel 18 miles at 50 mph. How long are you travelling for?

**Answer**

## Question 16

You are travelling at 65 mph for one hour and 10 minutes. How far do you travel?

**Answer**

## Question 17

You travel 120 miles in two hours. What speed are you travelling at?

**Answer**

## Question 18

You travel 80 miles at 50 mph. How long are you travelling for?

**Answer**

## Question 19

You are travelling at 40 mph for half an hour. How far do you travel?

**Answer**

## Question 20

You travel 80 miles in 1¾ of an hour. What speed are you travelling at?

**Answer**

## Question 21

You travel 35 miles at 70 mph. How long are you travelling for?

**Answer**

*Question 22*

You are travelling at 15 mph for 8 minutes. How far do you travel?

**Answer**

*Question 23*

You travel 16 miles in quarter of an hour. What speed are you travelling at?

**Answer**

*Question 24*

You travel 60 miles at 55 mph. How long are you travelling for?

**Answer**

*Question 25*

You travel 60 miles at 55 mph. How long are you travelling for?

**Answer**

*Question 26*

You travel 75 miles in one and half hours. What speed are you travelling at?

**Answer**

*Question 27*

You travel 1 mile at 60 mph. How long are you travelling for?

**Answer**

*Question 28*

You are travelling at 50 mph for 2 and half hours. How far do you travel?

**Answer**

*Question 29*

You travel 100 miles in 1 hour and 55 minutes. What speed are you travelling at?

**Answer**

## Question 30

You travel 600 miles at 80 mph. How long are you travelling for?

**Answer** ☐

## ANSWERS TO SPEED, DISTANCE AND TIME TEST

1.  35 miles
2.  30 mph
3.  36 mins
4.  112.5 miles
5.  56 mph
6.  3 hours
7.  146 miles
8.  30 mph
9.  1 hour 40 minutes
10. 15 miles
11. 79 mph
12. 51 mins
13. 20 miles
14. 68 mph
15. 21 minutes and 30 seconds
16. 76 miles
17. 60mph
18. 1 hour 36 mins
19. 20 miles
20. 46mph
21. 30 mins
22. 2 miles
23. 64mph
24. 1 hour 5 mins
25. 5 miles
26. 50mph
27. 1 minute
28. 125 miles
29. 52 mph
30. 7 hours 30 minutes

On the following pages I have provided you with a sample planning exercise for you to try. Give it a go and see how you get on. There is no time limit for this sample exercise.

## PLANNING EXERCISE - SEASIDE MISSION

You are the duty officer in charge at the Royal National Lifeboat Institution's (RNLI) rescue centre at FLITTERBY. The FLITTERBY lifeboat is currently involved in rescuing some sailors from a drifting yacht in the Irish Sea.

*It is exactly 10:00 am and the coxswain of the lifeboat has just radioed the following message to you:*

"One of the sailors we have taken off from the sinking yacht is desperately ill and must have a blood transfusion as soon as possible. I have just been talking, by radio, to the Accident & Emergency (A&E) staff at ASHBY hospital and they will be standing-by to receive him but have pointed out that every minute counts. Make sure the RNLI's ambulance (a specially adapted estate car) is ready to take him to the hospital as soon as we arrive at the jetty. I cannot give you an exact time of arrival, but it will not be before 10:20 hours, or later than 10:45 hours. Once we are tied up, it will take us 5 minutes to get him from the boat into the ambulance. It will be up to you to get him from the jetty to the A&E dept with the utmost urgency."

You study the map and recollect that there are 3 ways to get to hospital, each with advantages and disadvantages:

**1.** The route via the gate bridge is subject to delays as the crossings are controlled and the bridge is only open 3 times per hour for 12 minutes. The bridge is open at 10 minutes past, 30 minutes past and 10 minutes to the hour. The journey across the gate bridge will take you 10 minutes. The B120 is twisty and a maximum average speed could be no greater than 40 mph.

**2.** The route through the centre of ASHBY on the A424 is further but although it should be possible to average 40 mph out of town, once inside the central congestion zone, heavy traffic and narrow streets means no more than 5 mph can be averaged for the 10 miles through the walled part of the town. The one limitation from using the A424 is that from 11:00 hrs onwards the central congestion zone is very dense and traffic is at a standstill.

**3.** The new A11 by-pass is dual carriage and passes the hospital but, although the longest route, will allow averages of 70 mph to be achieved. It is possible to reach the A11 from FLITTERBY in 10 mins.

You warn the duty driver to stand-by. Unfortunately, you cannot alert the local police on the telephone to make any special arrangements, so there is no way of interrupting the steady but reliable timetable of the gate bridge. The duty officer at nearby RAF Valley tells you the Search and Rescue helicopter is unavailable as it is on a mission rescuing someone from an oil rig miles out to sea.

Your aim is to transport the sailor to the hospital in the quickest time possible.

## Question 1

How long in minutes will it take you to get from RNLI Flitterby to the A11 junction?

**Answer**

## Question 2

Based on the sailor arriving at Flitterby at the earliest time possible, what time will you reach the Hospital if you choose route 1?

**Answer**

## Question 3

Based on the sailor arriving at Flitterby at the latest time possible, what time will you reach the Hospital if you choose route 3?

**Answer**

## Question 4

Based on the sailor arriving at Flitterby at the latest time possible, what time will you reach the Hospital if you choose route 1?

**Answer**

## Question 5

Based on the sailor arriving at Flitterby at the earliest time possible, what time will you reach the Hospital if you choose route 2?

**Answer**

NOTE - You are to calculate the total journey times for each of the 3 different routes using Speed, Distance and Time calculations.

YOUR CALCULATIONS

**Remember:**

$$Speed = \frac{Distance}{Time}$$

$$Distance = Speed \times Time$$

$$Time = \frac{Distance}{Speed}$$

## SEASIDE MISSION SKETCH

ROAD TO A11 JUNCTION

RNLI FLITTERYBY

A11 BYPASS

A11 Junction

IRISH SEA

80 MILES   B120   A424   A11 BYPASS

90 MILES

RIVER ASHBY

GATE
BRIDGE

COASTAL LINE

ASHBY

40 MILES   B120

70 MILES

A424

280 MILES

H
ASHBY
HOSPITAL

A11 BYPASS

CENTRAL
CONGESTION ZONE
(The entire shaded area
is 10 miles in total)

## ANSWERS TO QUESTIONS

### Question 1

How long in minutes will it take you to get from RNLI Flitterby to the A11 junction?

ANSWER: 10 minutes

### Question 2

Based on the sailor arriving at Flitterby at the earliest time possible, what time will you reach the Hospital if you choose route 1?

The sailor arrives at Flitterby at 10:20hrs. It takes 5 minutes to load him into the ambulance which brings the time to 10:25hrs. It takes 10 minutes to get to the A11 junction which brings the time to 10:35hrs.

Travelling route 1, it is a total of 80 miles to the Gate Bridge. We are able to travel at a maximum speed of 40mph. To find out the time it takes to travel this distance we need to use the following calculation:

Time = Distance / Speed
Time = 80 / 40

ANSWER: 2 hours

We now know that we will arrive at the Gate Bridge at 12:35hrs. From the information provided we know that the Gate Bridge is open 3 times per hour for 12 minutes. The bridge is open at 10 minutes past, 30 minutes past and 10 minutes to the hour.

The bridge is already open when we arrive at 12:35 hours; therefore we are able to cross straight away. The journey across the gate bridge takes us 10 minutes, which means that we will arrive on the other side at 12:45hrs.

We now have to make the final journey along the B120 towards the hospital. The distance is 40 miles in total and we can travel at a maximum speed of 40 miles per hour. In order to calculate the time we need to use the following calculation:

Time = Distance / Speed
Time = 40 / 40

Answer = 1 hour

ANSWER: Arrive at the hospital at 13:45hrs.

## Question 3

Based on the sailor arriving at Flitterby at the latest time possible, what time will you reach the Hospital if you choose route 3?

The sailor arrives at Flitterby at 10:45hrs. It takes 5 minutes to load him into the ambulance which brings the time to 10:50hrs. It takes 10 minutes to get to the A11 junction which brings the time to 11:00hrs.

Travelling along route 3 we know that we can achieve a maximum speed of 70 miles per hour. In order to work out the total time it will take us to reach the hospital we need to use the following calculation:

Time = Distance / Speed
Time = 280 / 70
Answer = 4 hours

ANSWER: Arrive at the hospital will be 15:00hrs.

## Question 4

Based on the sailor arriving at Flitterby at the latest time possible, what time will you reach the Hospital if you choose route 1?

The sailor arrives at Flitterby at 10:45hrs. It takes 5 minutes to load him into the ambulance which brings the time to 10:50hrs. It takes 10 minutes to get to the A11 junction which brings the time to 11:00hrs.

Travelling route 1, it is a total of 80 miles to the Gate Bridge. We are able to travel at a maximum speed of 40mph. To find out the time it takes to travel this distance we need to use the following calculation:

Time = Distance / Speed
Time = 80 / 40
Answer = 2 hours

We now know that we will arrive at the Gate Bridge at 13:00hrs. From the information provided we know that the Gate Bridge is open 3 times per hour for 12 minutes. The bridge is open at 10 minutes past, 30 minutes past and 10 minutes to the hour.

The bridge is still open when we arrive at 13:00 hours; therefore we are able to cross straight away. The journey across the gate bridge takes us 10 minutes, which means that we will arrive on the other side at 13:10hrs.

We now have to make the final journey along the B120 towards the hospital.

The distance is 40 miles in total and we can travel at a maximum speed of 40 miles per hour. In order to calculate the time we need to use the following calculation:

Time = Distance / Speed
Time = 40 / 40
Answer = 1 hour

ANSWER: Arrive at the hospital at 14:10hrs.

## Question 5

Based on the sailor arriving at Flitterby at the earliest time possible, what time will you reach the Hospital if you choose route 2?

The sailor arrives at Flitterby at 10:20hrs. It takes 5 minutes to load him into the ambulance which brings the time to 10:25hrs. It takes 10 minutes to get to the A11 junction which brings the time to 10:35hrs.

We know that the distance from the A11 junction to the edge of the congestion zone is a total of 90 miles. We also know that the distance from the other side of the congestion zone to the hospital along the A424 is a total of 70 miles. Therefore we can add these two distances together to get a total distance (minus the congestion zone area) of 160 miles. In order to work out the time it takes to travel this distance we need to use the following calculation:

Time = Distance / Speed
Time = 160 / 40
Answer = 4 hours

We now need to work out the time it will take us to travel through the congestion zone. We know from the map that the distance inside the congestion zone is a total of 10 miles. We can only travel at a maximum speed of 5mph; therefore the calculation used to find out the total time it takes to travel through the congestion zone is as follows:

Time = Distance / Speed
Time = 10 / 5
Answer = 2 hours

All we need to do now is add the two travelling times together to reach a total of 6 hours travelling time.

ANSWER: Arrive at the hospital at 16:35hrs

## MORE SPEED, DISTANCE AND TIME QUESTIONS

There are 100 questions. You have 20 minutes to answer as many as possible. You are not permitted to use a calculator or write down your calculations. Work out the questions in your head.

**Q1.** At **4 mph**, how long does it take to travel **1 mile**?

**Q2.** At **120 mph**, how long does it take to travel **60 miles**?

**Q3.** At **30 mph**, how far do you travel in 1 hour and **36 mins**?

**Q4.** At **1 mph**, how long does it take to travel **15 miles**?

**Q5.** At **13 mph**, how long does it take to travel **13 miles**?

**Q6.** At **13 mph**, how long does it take to travel **13 miles**?

**Q7.** At **19 mph**, how long does it take to travel **19 miles**?

**Q8.** At **3 mph**, how long does it take to travel **11 miles**?

**Q9.** At **60 mph**, how far do you travel in **1 hour**?

**Q10.** At **36 mph**, how far do you travel in **15 mins**?

**Q11.** At **90 mph**, how long does it take to travel **12 miles**?

**Q12.** At **15 mph**, how long does it take to travel **40 miles**?

**Q13.** What speed covers **90 miles in 2 hours**?

**Q14.** At **165 mph**, how long does it take to travel **132 miles**?

**Q15.** At **19 mph**, how long does it take to travel **19 miles**?

**Q16.** What speed covers **20 miles in 2 hours**?

**Q17.** At **15 mph**, how long does it take to travel **88 miles**?

**Q18.** At **16 mph**, how far do you travel in **3 hours**?

**Q19.** At **72 mph**, how far do you travel in **25 mins**?

| | |
|---|---|
| **Q20.** At **38 mph**, how long does it take to travel **57 miles**? | |
| **Q21.** What speed covers **19 miles** in **1 hour**? | |
| **Q22.** At **156 mph**, how far do you travel in **1 hour**? | |
| **Q23.** At **200 mph**, how long does it take to travel **160 miles**? | |
| **Q24.** What speed covers **36 miles** in **1 hour**? | |
| **Q25** What speed covers **15 miles** in **15 hours**? | |
| **Q26.** What speed covers **3 miles** in **10 mins**? | |
| **Q27.** What speed covers **8 miles** in **24 mins**? | |
| **Q28.** At **80 mph**, how long does it take to travel **140 miles**? | |
| **Q29.** At **10 mph**, how long does it take to travel **10 miles**? | |
| **Q30.** At **170 mph**, how far do you travel in **1 hour**? | |
| **Q31.** At **20 mph**, how long does it take to travel **7 miles**? | |
| **Q32.** At **135 mph**, how long does it take to travel **72 miles**? | |
| **Q33.** What speed covers **18 miles** in **10 mins**? | |
| **Q34.** At **16 mph**, how long does it take to travel **12 miles**? | |
| **Q35.** At **2 mph**, how long does it take to travel **19 miles**? | |
| **Q36.** What speed covers **10 miles** in **1 hour and 15 mins**? | |
| **Q37.** At **16 mph**, how long does it take to travel **20 miles**? | |
| **Q38.** At **18 mph**, how long does it take to travel **180 miles**? | |
| **Q39.** What speed covers **80 miles** in **4 hours**? | |
| **Q40.** At **60 mph**, how long does it take to travel **120 miles**? | |
| **Q41.** At **80 mph**, how far do you travel in **27 mins**? | |

**Q42.** What speed covers **24 miles** in **2 hours and 24 mins**?

**Q43.** At **54 mph**, how long does it take to travel **18 miles**?

**Q44.** What speed covers **48 miles** in **15 mins**?

**Q45.** At **10 mph**, how long does it take to travel **12 miles**?

**Q46.** What speed covers **45 miles** in **1 hour and 40 mins**?

**Q47.** At **100 mph**, how far do you travel in **18 mins**?

**Q48.** What speed covers **2 miles in 20 mins**?

**Q49.** At **44 mph**, how far do you travel in **6 hours and 15 mins**?

**Q50.** At **5 mph**, how long does it take to travel **5 miles**?

**Q51.** What speed covers **14 miles in 2 hours**?

**Q52.** What speed covers **15 miles** in **2 hours and 30 mins**?

**Q53.** What speed covers **6 miles** in **1 hour and 30 mins**?

**Q54.** What speed covers **15 miles** in **45 mins**?

**Q55.** At **20 mph**, how far do you travel in **3 hours and 15 mins**?

**Q56.** At **18 mph**, how far do you travel in **20 mins**?

**Q57.** At 16 mph, how far do you travel in 1 hour and 15 mins?

**Q58.** What speed covers **2 miles** in **40 mins**?

**Q59.** What speed covers **8 miles** in **1 hour**?

**Q60.** What speed covers **11 miles** in **1 hour**?

**Q61.** What speed covers **6 miles** in **10 mins**?

**Q62.** What speed covers **25 miles** in **10 mins**?

**Q63.** What speed covers **28 miles** in **16 mins**?

**Q64.** At **10 mph,** how far do you travel in **6 mins?**

**Q65.** What speed covers **14 miles** in **1 hour and 24 mins?**

**Q66.** At **8 mph,** how far do you travel in **4 hours?**

**Q67.** What speed covers **14 miles** in **2 hours?**

**Q68.** At **28 mph,** how long does it take to travel **84 miles?**

**Q69.** At **15 mph,** how far do you travel in **1 hour and 20 mins?**

**Q70.** At **5 mph,** how long does it take to travel **16 miles?**

**Q71.** What speed covers **14 miles** in **2 hours?**

**Q72.** What speed covers **40 miles** in **8 hours?**

**Q73.** At **6 mph,** how long does it take to travel **6 miles?**

**Q74.** At **30 mph,** how long does it take to travel **28 miles?**

**Q75.** What speed covers **15 miles** in **3 hours?**

**Q76.** What speed covers **6 miles** in **45 mins?**

**Q77.** What speed covers **4 miles** in **20 mins?**

**Q78.** At **12 mph,** how far do you travel in **2 hours?**

**Q79.** At **17 mph,** how long does it take to travel **17 miles?**

**Q80.** What speed covers **34 miles** in **24 mins?**

**Q81.** At **36 mph,** how long does it take to travel **15 miles?**

**Q82.** What speed covers **57 miles** in **9 hours and 30 mins?**

**Q83.** At **68 mph,** how far do you travel in **1 hour?**

**Q84.** What speed covers **8 miles** in **6 mins?**

**Q85.** At **19 mph,** how long does it take to travel **76 miles?**

| | |
|---|---|
| **Q86.** At **117 mph**, how far do you travel in **1 hour and 40 mins**? | |
| **Q87.** At **27 mph**, how far do you travel in **1 hour and 20 mins**? | |
| **Q88.** At **8 mph**, how long does it take to travel **8 miles**? | |
| **Q89.** At **6 mph**, how far do you travel in **21 hours and 20 mins**? | |
| **Q90.** At **7 mph**, how far do you travel in **2 hours**? | |
| **Q91.** What speed covers **84 miles** in **36 mins**? | |
| **Q92.** At **16 mph**, how far do you travel in **6 hours and 15 mins**? | |
| **Q93.** What speed covers **19 miles** in **1 hour**? | |
| **Q94.** At **36 mph**, how long does it take to travel **120 miles**? | |
| **Q95.** What speed covers **13 miles** in **1 hour**? | |
| **Q96.** At **9 mph**, how far do you travel in **1 hour and 20 mins**? | |
| **Q97.** What speed covers **15 miles** in **12 mins**? | |
| **Q98.** What speed covers **11 miles** in **15 mins**? | |
| **Q99.** What speed covers **14 miles** in **1 hour and 10 mins**? | |
| **Q100.** At **44 mph**, how long does it take to travel **44 miles**? | |

## ANSWERS

1. 15 mins
2. 30 mins
3. 48 miles
4. 15 hours
5. 1 hour
6. 1 hour
7. 1 hour
8. 3 hours & 40 mins
9. 60 miles
10. 9 miles
11. 8 mins
12. 2 hours & 40 mins
13. 45 mph
14. 48 mins
15. 1 hour
16. 10 mph
17. 5 hours & 52 mins
18. 48 miles
19. 30 miles
20. 1 hour & 30 mins
21. 19 mph
22. 156 miles
23. 48 mins
24. 36 mph
25. 1 mph
26. 18 mph
27. 20 mph
28. 1 hour & 45 mins
29. 1 hour
30. 170 miles
31. 21 mins
32. 32 mins
33. 108 mph
34. 45 mins

35. 9 hours & 30 mins
36. 8 mph
37. 1 hour & 15 mins
38. 10 hours
39. 20 mph
40. 2 hours
41. 36 miles
42. 10 mph
43. 20 mins
44. 192 mph
45. 1 hour & 12 mins
46. 27 mph
47. 30 miles
48. 6 mph
49. 275 miles
50. 1 hour
51. 7 mph
52. 6 mph
53. 4 mph
54. 20 mph
55. 65 miles
56. 6 miles
57. 20 miles
58. 3 mph
59. 8 mph
60. 11 mph
61. 36 mph
62. 150 mph
63. 105 mph
64. 1 miles
65. 10 mph
66. 32 miles
67. 7 mph
68. 3 hours

69. 20 miles
70. 3 hours & 12 mins
71. 7 mph
72. 5 mph
73. 1 hour
74. 56 mins
75. 5 mph
76. 8 mph
77. 12 mph
78. 24 miles
79. 1 hour
80. 85 mph
81. 25 mins
82. 6 mph
83. 68 miles
84. 80 mph
85. 4 hours
86. 195 miles
87. 36 miles
88. 1 hour
89. 128 miles
90. 14 miles
91. 140 mph
92. 100 miles
93. 19 mph
94. 3 hours & 20 mins
95. 13 mph
96. 2 miles
97. 75 mph
98. 44 mph
99. 12 mph
100. 1 hour

# CHAPTER 7

# HOW TO PASS ARMY OFFICER SELECTION BOARD INTERVIEWS

## HOW TO PASS THE PARACHUTE REGIMENT OFFICER INTERVIEWS

During this section of the guide I will provide you with a number of sample interview questions and advice on how to answer them. Whilst some of the questions will appear to be easy to answer, it is still important that we cover them, in order to ensure that you are fully prepared. I also recommend that you re-visit the ACA interview section of the guide, as some of the questions asked may be duplicated during the AOSB.

I have divided the sample questions into various different sections to assist you during your preparation.

## Section 1 – Personal/CV questions

Q. When and where were you born?

Q. Where are you living now and who are you living with?

Q. Where else have you lived apart from with your parents?

Q. Describe your home life to me?

Q. What was your life like growing up?

**TIPS:** Questions that relate to your home life are designed to assess how stable you are as person, whether or not you have any responsibilities at home, whether you are generally a happy person and also what you have learnt from life's experiences to date.

> Know key dates of where you have lived.

> Know key dates of your CV

> Try and provide examples of where you have moved around. This demonstrates that you are flexible and adaptable when the need arises.

> It is preferable that your home life is stable.

> The more responsibilities you have at home, such as washing, ironing, cleaning, financial responsibilities the better.

> If you have lived with other people, apart from your immediate family, tell them so. Remember – as an Army Officer you will be living with men and women of different ages etc.

## Education

Q. How many schools have you attended and what years did you attend them?

Q. What did you think about your teachers?

Q. Tell me about your exam results; did you achieve the grades you wanted?

Q. Could you have worked harder whilst at school?

**TIPS:** although these are relatively easy questions to respond to, ones that relate to your exam results and how hard you worked whilst at school could catch you out. You have to be honest about your results. If they were not up to the standard that you expected, have a valid reason why. Never be disrespectful of your teachers or the educational system. Remember that you are applying to join a disciplined service.

## School/college

Q. Did you learn anything from other students?

Q. Did you have any responsibilities whilst at school or college?

Q. What sports did you participate in whilst at school or college?

Q. What clubs or societies were you a member of?

Q. Do you have the Duke of Edinburgh or similar awards?

Q. Where did you travel with school?

Q. Did you have any gaps in your education?

**TIPS:** If you did have any gaps in your education, it is better to say that you used the time wisely. Maybe you went travelling around the world in order to gain new experiences and cultures, or maybe you wanted to take time out from your studies to take on a work related role or even a charity role. Whatever you do, do not say that you did nothing with your time off. If you went travelling, what did you gain from the experience?

Whilst at school or college it would be an advantage if you had some level of responsibility. For example, maybe you were a prefect or head of year, or maybe you were the captain of a sports team. You are applying to become an Officer, which effectively means you are going to be a manager and a leader. Having some previous experience of these important roles will be an advantage. If you haven't had any responsibilities in your life to date, how do you know that you'll be a good leader or manager in the Parachute Regiment?

## Outside interests and hobbies

Q. What sports are you currently engaged in?

Q. What sporting achievements have you gained?

Q. Have you been part of any youth organisations such as the Cadet, Scouts, Guides or Sea Cadets?

Q. Describe your hobbies and interests?

Q. Are you currently employed either full-time or part-time?

Q. What did you used to do during your school holidays?

Q. Have you ever travelled? If so, where and when did you go and what did you gain from the experience(s)?

Q. What are you future ambitions or plans?

**TIPS:** It is imperative that you demonstrate during the interview that you are an active person. If you sit at home all evening on your computer, playing games and surfing the net, then you are probably not the type of person the Army are looking for. Demonstrate to the interviewer that you are active, a team player and have hobbies and interests that challenge you both mentally and physically.

## Employment

Q. What jobs have you had to date?

Q. What responsibilities did you have during each job?

Q. Why did you leave each job?

Q. Did you complete any courses or gain any qualifications during each job?

Q. Who did you have to communicate with in each job?

Q. Were you part of a team or did you work alone?

Q. What were your appraisals like?

**TIPS:** If you have no experience in a work related role to date, how do you know that you will be a good employee for the Army/Parachute Regiment? Make sure you have some work experience under your belt, even if it's part time work or charity work. Try to also provide examples of responsibilities during each work role and any managerial experience too. These will all work in your favour.

## Motivational questions

Q. Why do you want to join the Army? Have you considered the RAF or the Royal Navy?

Q. What specifically attracts you to the Parachute Regiment?

Q. When did you first want to join the Army/Parachute Regiment and has anyone influenced you in your decision to join?

Q. Who have you talked to about a career in the Parachute Regiment?

Q. How many visits have you had to the Armed Forces Careers Office?

Q. Have you previously attended AOSB? If you have, what have you done to improve on last time?

Q. What contact have you had with the Army? Have you visited any establishments or spoken to any serving members?

Q. Are there any disadvantages for you joining the Parachute Regiment?

Q. What do your family and friends think of you joining?

Q. Why have you applied to join the Parachute Regiment?

Q. Will you join as a regular Para soldier if you are unsuccessful as an Officer?

Q. Would you consider any other branches/regiments of the Army other than the Parachute Regiment?

Q. What research have you carried out during your preparation for joining the Parachute Regiment?

Q. What length of commission/service would you like to work?

Q. What qualities are required in order to become a Parachute Regiment Officer?

**TIPS:** Defend your decision to join the Parachute Regiment as an Officer as much as possible and state that you do not want to become a regular soldier. In order to be capable of achieving this, you will need to know the Regiment inside out. Make sure you research key information about the Parachute Regiment and also the Army in general.

## *Knowledge of the Army and the Parachute Regiment*

Q. Tell me what you know about the history of the Army?

Q. Tell me what you know about the history of the Parachute Regiment?

Q. What training will you undergo as an Officer?

Q. Do you think you will have any problems or face any challenges during Officer Initial Training?

Q. Have you learnt anything about other branches of the Army?

Q. What is the main role of the Parachute Regiment?

Q. Tell me what you know about the different aircrafts that serve in the Army?

Q. Tell me what you know about the different types of weapons that the Army/Parachute Regiment employs?

Q. How would you feel about going to war?

Q. Where are the UK bases of the Army?

Q. Where is the Parachute Regiment based in the UK?

Q. What current operations is the Parachute Regiment currently involved in?

Q. Whereabouts in the world are the wider Army operating right now?

Q. Do you know the Parachute Regiment charter?

## THE PARACHUTE REGIMENT CHARTER

"What manner of men are these who wear the maroon red beret? They are firstly all volunteers, and are then toughened by hard physical training. As a result they have that infectious optimism and that offensive eagerness which comes from physical well being. They have jumped from the air and by doing so have conquered fear. Their duty lies in the van of the battle: they are proud of this honour and have never failed in any task. They have the highest standards in all things, whether it be skill in battle or smartness in the execution of all peace time duties. They have shown themselves to be as tenacious and determined in defence as they are courageous in attack. They are, in fact, men apart - every man an Emperor."

- FIELD MARSHAL THE VISCOUNT MONTGOMERY OF ALAMEIN

### Current affairs questions

Current affairs are a very important area of your preparation. You must carry out plenty of research in relation to current affairs. Not only will you need it during the interview(s), but it will also assist you during the essay element of the AOSB.

Here are a few important tips to help you research current affairs effectively:

*Tip 1* – Be careful what paper(s) you read. The type of paper you read will reflect you as a person. If you tell the interviewer that you are an avid reader of the Sun or the Daily Star, you may not be Officer material. In the build up to AOSB, try reading the Times, or another quality newspaper.

*Tip 2* – I would strongly recommend that you subscribe to 'The Week'. This is a fantastic journal that will break down the week's stories for you. This will save having to buy lots of different newspapers.

You can subscribe to the week at the following website:

www.theweek.co.uk

*Tip 3* – Consider reading the Economist. Once again, this is a quality journal that will provide you with lots of current affairs information.

You can subscribe to the Economist at the following website:

www.economist.com

*Tip 4* – Don't just research affairs that are relevant to the Army or the Armed Forces in general. Other topics are just as important such as the Olympics or the World Cup. Try to think about what is topical at the moment. Write down a list of issues affecting the world right now and read up on them.

The purpose of the current affairs section of the AOSB interview is designed to assess how informed you are of current global affairs. You should have a general view on each subject and have an understanding of why the issue is important. Try to have a general view of the whole world with knowledge of a number of issues and events.

Use this format to help you research news and current affairs events:

• What is the subject?

• Why is it significant?

• What is your opinion on it?

*Tip 5* – Read the Pegasus Journal. Pegasus is the Regimental Journal of the Parachute Regiment and is published three times a year with two Journals and one Yearbook. The yearbook is now dedicated to the Parachute Regimental Association and the Journals also carry important PRA news as well as Obituaries and Last Post.

You can subscribe and obtain back copies of the journal by the following means:

In writing

*Subscriptions Manager*
PEGASUS JOURNAL
Regimental Headquarters
The Parachute Regiment
Merville Barracks
Circular Road South
Colchester
Essex CO2 7UT

By telephone:
Subscriptions Manager:
(01206) 817088

By e mail:
pegasusjournal@btconnect.com

## SAMPLE CURRENT AFFAIRS QUESTIONS

**Q.** Take me on a tour of the world and tell me what's caught your eye in the news recently.

**Q.** Tell me about 6 current affairs from abroad and six from home.

**Q.** Tell me about a news story from each continent.

## USEFUL WEBSITES

BBC News: www.bbc.co.uk/news/

The Times Online: www.timesonline.co.uk

NATO (North Atlantic Treaty Organisation: www.nato.int

Ministry of Defence: www.mod.uk

Army: www.army.mod.uk

Royal Navy: www.royalnavy.mod.uk

Royal Air Force: www.raf.mod.uk

## FINAL INTERVIEW TIPS

• Research key affairs from across the world.

• Have a broad knowledge of current affairs.

• Research affairs that have happened in the last 12 months.

• Focus in detail on events in the last 6 month.

• Select 6 topics for 'home' affairs (e.g. the budget, gang culture).

• Select 6 topics for 'away' affairs. Make sure that you use examples from right across the world.

• Gauge an opinion of each affair (you will need to be able to argue your point).

• Know key facts: people, numbers, locations etc.

• A firm handshake demonstrates a lot about your character.

• Be to the point and concise (don't waffle).

• Hold even eye contact with each boarding officer.

• Avoid hesitations such as "erm, ah, umm etc".

- Don't use slang.
- Sit up straight and don't slouch.
- Be confident but not overly so!
- Learn the dates and events listed on your application form.
- Make yourself stand out - do something different.
- Be aware of your weaknesses.
- Identify your strengths.
- Think before you speak.

A FEW FINAL WORDS

You have now reached the end of the guide and no doubt you will be ready to start preparing for the Parachute Regiment selection process. Just before you go off and start on your preparation, consider the following.

The majority of candidates who pass the selection process have a number of common factors. These are as follows:

### 1. They believe in themselves.

The first factor is self-belief. Regardless of what anyone tells you, you can pass the selection process and you can achieve high scores. Just like any job of this nature, you have to be prepared to work hard in order to be successful. The biggest piece of advice I can give you is to concentrate on matching the assessable qualities that form part of the scoring criteria. These would be at the forefront of my mind if I was going through selection right now. Make sure you have the self-belief to pass the selection process and fill your mind with positive thoughts.

### 2. They prepare fully.

The second factor is preparation. Those people who achieve in life prepare fully for every eventuality and that is what you must do when you apply to become an Officer with the Parachute Regiment. Work very hard and especially concentrate on your weak areas. Within this guide I have spoken a lot about preparation. Identify the areas that you are weak on and go all out to improve them.

### 3. They persevere.

Perseverance is a fantastic word. Everybody comes across obstacles or setbacks in their life, but it is what you do about those setbacks that is important. If you fail at something, then ask yourself 'why' have I failed? This will allow you to improve for next time and if you keep improving and trying, success will eventually follow. Apply this same method of thinking when you apply to join the Parachute Regiment as an Officer.

### 4. They are self-motivated.

How much do you want to join the Parachute Regiment? Do you want it, or do you really want it? When you apply to join you should want it more than anything in the world. Your levels of self motivation will shine through when you walk into the AFCO and when you attend the Army Officer Selection

Board. For the weeks and months leading up to the selection process, be motivated as best you can and always keep your fitness levels up as this will serve to increase your levels of motivation.

Work hard, stay focused and be what you want...

*Richard McMunn*

Richard McMunn

P.S. Come and spend a day with my team on the one day intensive Army Officer AOSB preparation course at the following website:

**www.ArmyOfficerCourse.co.uk**

**Visit www.how2become.co.uk to find more
titles and courses that will help you to pass the
Parachute Regiment selection process, including:**

• How to pass the Army Officer interview.

• 1 Day Army Officer training course.

• Online Army Officer psychometric testing.

• Psychometric testing books and CD's.

www.how2become.co.uk